V11
BOOK OF
LIVED

Penny Authors

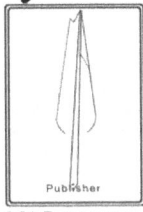

MA PUBLISHER

Penny Authors

Copyright © Penny Authors 2025

Produced by MAPublisher for Penny Authors
Email: Pennyauthors@yahoo.co.uk
www.pennyauthors.org.uk

Published by MA Publishing (Penzance)
Email: mapublisher@yahoo.com
www.mapublisher.org.uk

Address
14 Adelaide Street
Penzance, Cornwall, TR18 2ER

Released on August 2025

Printed in the region the books have been published: Australia | Canada | Europe | UK | USA

ISBN-13: 9781915958334

All rights reserved. No part of this publication may be reproduced, stored in a retrieval system, or transmitted, in any form or by any means, electronic, mechanical, photocopying, recording, public performances or otherwise, without prior written permission of the copyright holder, except for brief quotations embodied in critical articles or reviews.

Disclaimer:
All expressions and opinions of the work belong to the artists/poets, and PA does not share or endorse any other than to provide the open platform to publish their work. For further information on PA policies please email: pennyauthors@yahoo.co.uk for further information and submission guidelines.

Cover designed by Mayar Akash
Typeset in Times Roman

 Paper printed on is FSC Certified, lead free, acid free, buffered paper made from wood-based pulp. Our paper meets the ISO 9706 standard for permanent paper. As such, paper will last several hundred years when stored.

Testimonials

"I really want to thank you for all of your encouragement and kindness about my poetry, without which I am sure I wouldn't have had the confidence to keep writing."

Chloe Hall, Tavistock, Devon, UK

"Never in my wildest dreams did I ever think my poetry would be published, I didn't think it was ever good enough. But a chance conversation set the wheels in motion and in the space of just over a month I found out about Penny Authors, submitted my poetry and now I have 4 published in the latest Anthology and it's madness. I can't recommend Penny Authors enough for giving people a chance and a voice!!!"

Gary Curson, Newquay, Cornwall, UK

"This has left me speechless & I can't wait to meet you at the book launch. The perfect prescription to carry on & finish my goal in releasing a book of my poetry. Thank you for this Mayar!"

Tyrone Warren, St Buryan, Cornwall, UK

"I'll do my best to make you proud, I'm going to get back to writing"

(Late) Stuart "Coopsie" Cooper, Penzance, Cornwall, UK

"Thank you so much for the list of poems that will be published in the next anthology. How exciting that it will be published in July - that's a lot sooner than we thought!"
Clare Saunders Whiting, Ponsanooth, Cornwall, UK

Roll Call

We at Penny Authors like to recognise, remind and remember all the Penny Authors that have taken part past always and present:

1. Mayar Akash (Founder)
2. Zainab Khan,
3. Paul Harvey,
4. Isaac Harvey,
5. Rebekah Vaughan,
6. Rabia Mehmood,
7. Tamanna Parveen,
8. Ellis Dixon-King,
9. Liam Newton,
10. Prof. Md Nurul Huque,
11. Kalam Choudhury,
12. Rashma Mehta,
13. Matthew Saunders Whiting
14. Akik Miah
15. Nirmal Kaur
16. Julie Archbold
17. Lora Ashman
18. John Robert Gordon
19. Julie Anne Wheeler
20. Late Joan Hodge
21. Ruth Lewarne
22. Bhupendra M. Gandhi
23. Nicki & Laura Ellis
24. Alga Statham
25. Jeremy J. Lovelady
26. Peter Fox
27. Jamal Hasan
28. Stephan Goldsmith
29. Clare Saunders Whiting
30. Sally Walker
31. Elsa Kiernanfox
32. Jaida Begum
33. Abdul Mannan
34. John Cynddylan Dillon
35. Suzette Reed
36. Sandra Sanjeet Green
37. Coral Dodsworth
38. Chris York
39. Amitrajit Raajan
40. Ossian Hughes
41. Stuart Cooper
42. Mustak Mustafa
43. Samiul Fox
44. Ayesha Chowdhury
45. Ferdous Rahman
46. Abu Maryam Gous
47. Steve Willoughby
48. Abul Hussain
49. Libby Pentreath
50. Paul Phillips
51. Adrian Smith
52. Paul Crump
53. Roger Lowry
54. Moriom Chaudhury
55. David Harley
56. John S. Wallis
57. Michael Ashton
58. Sabina Begum
59. Mary Fletcher
60. Rob Kersley
61. Tyrone M Warren
62. Alison Ali Norton
63. Andrew Harry
64. Janey Bryson
65. Paul Keeting
66. Res John Burman
67. Robyn Harry
68. Jade Carter-Bennet
69. Leo Rudman
70. Opu Islam
71. Eve Wakeling
72. Edwin Lewis
73. Tahi Chowdhury
74. Jenny Bishop

75. Angie Butler
76. Adrian Frost
77. Vivian Pedley
78. Robert Spencer
79. Pam Turner
80. Leema Begum
81. Chloe Hall
82. Keith Woodhouse
83. Alan S Whitfield
84. Sonja Fairfield
85. Daniel Munn
86. Penny Collins
87. Julie Flowerdew
88. Rosie Beale
89. Carol Bea
90. Ruth Husbands
91. Neil Graham Oats
92. Joanna Edwards
93. Antony Craig Oats
94. Bea Thompson
95. Nayma Chumchoun
96. Jonathan Hayter
97. Mukut Borpujari
98. Francesca Owen
99. Lowenna H. Kaute
100. Valerie Kaute
101. Christine Jilbert
102. Nicole Paton
103. Errol Powel
104. Graham Rhodes
105. Mary E. Down
106. Gary Curson
107. Derrick J Hardy
108. Keith Lesser
109. Matthew Hill
110. Thomas D. Lynas
111. Loretta Gray
112. Jack Bennet
113. Sarah Turner
114. Nete Kroell
115. Anthony Mathews
116. John Pestle
117. Ian "Spud" Stride
118. Aurora Cawte
119. Michelle Berry
120. Jonathan Coudrille
121. Perwein Shah
122. Suzanne E. Phillips
123. Dan Foreman
124. Ashiqa Rahman
125. Gret Woodason
126. Andrew Dingly
127. Nazia Noman
128. Dawn G. Whiting

What is new this year?

What happens for penny authors page
In the 2025, volume 11, there is more information about what happens for "Penny Authors" what is already in place.

Index page
We have a fully integrated "index" in the back – thus making it clear, where who's poems are in the book.

Dedication Page
We have dedication page – clearly outlining the purpose of "Penny Authors" and expressing gratitude.

Acknowledgement page
Acknowledgement page, this is to thank those that have been supporting Penny Authors'.

Testimonial page
Celebrate our Penny Authors who have benefitted from this experience

Review page
To recap on what has happened in and since the previous publication.

Dedication

For those who lived, and those who loved them.

This volume is dedicated to every soul who offered a piece of their lived truth to the archive. To the quiet ones who wrote in the margins, the bold ones who spoke in thunder, and the departed whose echoes still shape our breath—we honour you.

To the contributors:
Your words are not just remembered. They are kept.
Not just published. They are prayed over.
Not just read. They are received with reverence.

To the communities that raised these voices, and the hands that held them through grief, joy, and becoming—this book is yours too.

To the Divine, who called this work into being:
May this offering be worthy. May it serve. May it love.

And to those who will one day find these pages and feel less alone—
We wrote this for you.

Acknowledgement

This anthology was not made alone.

It was shaped by the breath of many—those who wrote, those who remembered, those who held space for the living and the lost. Every poem, every testimony, every anonymous offering carries the weight of love, grief, and devotion. We acknowledge the courage it takes to speak, and the grace it takes to listen.

To everyone who published with Penny Authors over the year—those who returned, and those who never left us—thank you. Your presence is a blessing, your words a legacy.

To Suzette Reed, who championed me to continue:
Your faith lit the path when I could not see it. Thank you for believing in the promise.

To John Cyndylan, Angie Butler, Rob Kersley, Zainab Khan, Paul Harvey, Liam Newton, and Isaac Harvey:
Thank you for your trust. Your belief in this work gave it breath. You are part of its foundation.

To the communities behind each voice:
Thank you for your quiet labour, your encouragement, your rituals of care. You are the unseen editors of this work.

To those who departed before this volume was born:
You are present in every page. We name you in silence, and we carry your memory forward.

To God—Divinity—who gave me a second chance to deliver my promise:
I acknowledge the sacredness of this task. May my stewardship be faithful. Long may I serve those who hear the calling to have their spirit championed through words—and I publish.

And to every reader who arrives with tenderness—
You are part of this circle now. Welcome.

Foreword

By the Curator

There are books that entertain.
There are books that inform.
And then there are books that remember.

The Book of Lived is one such book.

This volume is not curated for prestige or perfection. It is curated for truth. For courage. For the quiet voices that often go unheard. It is a space where grief is not edited out, where joy is not polished for performance, and where every poet—regardless of background, age, or experience—is welcomed with dignity.

As curator, I have had the privilege of reading every submission, witnessing the rawness, the rhythm, the resistance. I have seen poems that tremble with pain, others that shine with resilience, and many that do both. I have seen poets write through illness, through injustice, through memory and myth. I have seen love—fierce, maternal, romantic, divine—threaded through these pages like lifelines.

This anthology is not just a publication. It is a community. A movement. A mirror. It is built on the belief that every voice matters, and that poetry is not a luxury—it is a necessity.

To the contributors: thank you for your trust.
To the readers: thank you for your presence.
To the future Penny Authors: we are waiting for you.

Let this book be a testament.
Let it be a torch.
Let it be a place where you feel seen.

With gratitude,
Mayar Akash
Curator, *Volume 11: The Book of Lived*

CONTENT

Testimonials	3
Roll Call	4
What Is New This Year?	6
Dedication	7
Acknowledgement	8
The Book Of Lived	9
Introduction	13
New Beginnings	15
The Seagull's Cry	16
For Mothers	17
Stranger On A Page	18
Purpose	19
Eid's Silent Shadows	20
Joy Found Me Dancing	21
Hooves. A Love Story	22
A Father's Love That Endures	23
Moved On	24
Missed Moments	25
Rekindled Bonds	26
Taunts	27
Ascea	28
The Friend Who Wasn't	29
In Pursuit	31
Two Brains, One Battle From The Body Of A Survivor	32
Little By Little	34
Getting Up In The Morning	35
I Am Not What Happened	36
I Fell Again	37
Let It Pass	38
The Alarm Clock – I	39
A Pocketful Of Paradise.	40
What If...	41
I'm Worthy, I'm Enough.	42
Sweet Baby	43
Nothing To See Here	44
On An Ancient Face Is Inscribed	47
Strings Attached	48
We Are Dust	51
Interesting &Possible	52
Legacy	53
Natural Love	55

Bodmin Moor	56
True, Authentic Self	57
Woke	58
Belief	59
An Island Home Of Light	60
Indra's Net	61
Today, Without Warning, I Enter The Lion's Den	62
Gaza Haiku	63
Your Song Reaches The Laughing Leaves	64
Trapped	65
The Well Of St Morwenna	66
The Falling Leaves Of Autumn	68
The Passing Of The Wind: Aka The Prezident Erected	69
United States Of Israel	70
To A Lost Wild Beauty.	71
Once Upon A Time....	72
By Leema Begum	72
Self Knowledge	73
Tango Dream	74
Once Upon A Time – Empty House	75
By Leema Begum	75
Come With Me	76
Don't Buy Me Flowers	77
Poets	79
Music	80
Waiting For The Summer	82
Lost And Found	83
Always Know That I Still Matter	84
The Love That Grows	85
A Lonely Child With Skies Of Blue	86
If I Hurry Up The Hill	87
Run Melania Run Blues	88
Blue Sky	89
Voices In Silence	90
Lonely Man	91
A Bloody Bangladesh	92
For Steve	93
A Cry For Justice	94
Is It Too Late	95
Self-Respect:	96
If Princess Anne	97
Amazonian Alexa	98
The Way I Love My Matty Dread	99

No Answers	100
The Stillness	101
Time Passes	102
Other Women	103
North London Nightlife	104
It's No Walk In The Park	105
The Gurney	106
Friendship	107
Yellow Metal & The Solitary Glove	108
The Question	109
Animal Tongue	110
Look Elsewhere	111
Autumn	112
I Dreamt Of You	113
Birthday Treat – Bodmin Jail	114
Celebrating Honeybees	115
What's Happening To Me	116
Summer Is Here	117
Mounts Bay	118
Beneath The Silent Waves	119
Redemption	120
As The Wind Rised	122
Elavéne's Lament	123
True Talk	126
Only A Certain Breed	127
School Life	129
By Leema Begum	129
Love	130
Tony Blair	131
Boris Johnson	133
You Never Know	132
Leave Something	133
Big Brother Matty	135
Index	136
What Happens For Penny Authors?	139
Social & Media Presence:	141
Votes & Ratings	149
The Last Words	154
Forever Growing!	154
Invitation To Volume 12	155
Synopsis	156

Introduction

Welcome to *Volume 11: The Book of Lived*—a living archive of truth, memory, and poetic witness. This anthology is not just a collection of poems. It is a gathering of voices. A ledger of survival. A map of experience. Every poem here is a footprint. Every voice, a light.

So much happens in Penny Authors that everyone has a place, a spot to fit in—and some. This volume is the result of that ethos: inclusive, celebratory, and ever-growing. It brings together poets from all walks of life—young and old, seasoned and new, grieving and rejoicing. What unites them is the courage to speak, the generosity to share, and the refusal to be silent.

Here you will find poems of healing and heartbreak, protest and prayer, laughter and lament. Some will whisper. Some will roar. All will live.

Penny Authors is more than a platform—it is a gateway, a community, a legacy. Every contributor is honoured. Every voice is valued. Every poem is part of something larger than itself. As a Penny Author, you are not just published—you are registered in the British Library, featured in print, profiled online, and invited to participate in radio, YouTube, peer review, and public recitals. You are part of a movement.

We encourage you to:

- Share your work proudly
- Champion another poet
- Build your anthology library
- Recite your poems aloud
- Vote and review your peers
- Leave something behind that cannot be erased

This is a space where kindness matters, where truth is welcomed, and where your voice—however quiet or bold—is heard.

We invite you to read slowly. To listen deeply. To carry these voices with you. And if you feel moved—write your own. *Volume 12* is waiting.

This is *The Book of Lived*.
And you are part of it.

Penny Authors

New Beginnings

Now I realize I am free,
a free busy bee,
I can come and go as I please,
and learn a lot of amazing new things.

Here is my life a new chapter dawn,
the world is my oyster,
so, let's begin and re learn,
all the past failed education update and set your sights
on a first-year apprentice degree.
My company agrees.

Here I am at nearly the end,
another journey,
took me through the years of isolation, covid,
a focus to move life forward,
hopefully something new and exciting awaits.

Proves it's never too late.

The Seagull's Cry

The sea gulls' cry circles the air,
calls to the skies for attention,
wakes up the weary from tossed hours of torment,
screams of life, and love and strength and salvation.

Relentless as the waves which carry them,
never ending like the winds that effortlessly bear their weight,
timeless as love and longing,
reminders that life will go on.

Reminders that life will go on.

For Mothers

You are beautiful and kind,
you will be with us all the time,
in our hearts and our minds,
as we walk the roads of time.

You gave us your love,
you gave us your joy,
your zest for life, and so much more.
Nothing was too much trouble,
you were there for each one of us,
you give up your time, in a flash,
helped every one of us out, children,
grandchildren and great grandchildren too,
one special person through and through.
As you go on your journey, with a peaceful mind,
a place where there is no sorrow or pain,
only warmth and love.

You will meet up with your family of loved ones again,
where the sun shines and its warmth are a pleasure to behold,
birds, butterflies and the honeybees, rabbits galore,
nature at its best,
and you are ready for your lovely peaceful rest.

Night, night, my mum love from us all.

Loving poem for mothers.

Stranger On A Page

Sitting reading words,
in the silence of your mind,
sitting reading words,
something stirs from deep inside,

Something strikes a chord,
something feels familiar,
something feels so real,
something drags you deeper.

The more that you read,
the more you seem to know,
a connection being made,
a connection starts to grow,

Tt's written by a stranger,
a stranger on a page,
a stranger you don't know,
yet, their words strike home,

The more you sit and read,
the more you seem to know,
just how this person feels,
but how can it be so?

You've never even met them,
their name you do not know.
For they are just a stranger
a stranger on a page.

Purpose

I walk on the path to nowhere,
to find my purpose,
and to reach somewhere,
keep walking on,
and on,
It may take years before the calm,
your mind doesn't give up,
fills your head,
no let up.

"Stop!"
I shout!
Stop!

Let it all out,
Let it go,
That cold north wind blows.

A nip to your ear,
A whisper of a song,
Very music from your soul listen.
Can you hear?

Sit alone staring out at nature
as far as the eye can see
Beauty and peace let it be,
Let it be.

A silence falls
just the breeze and the beauty of it all,
t's a perfect, a picture of the living world,
most Will never truly see,
and live, to feel truly free.

Eid's Silent Shadows

On Eid, no place for us to go,
no family love, just feelings of low.

Arguments brewed in festive air,
my mother's sorrow, my stepdad's despair.

Each Eid felt grim, a time to dread,
my friends would share their joyful day,
with family close, in celebration's way.

Their laughter echoed through the world outside,
while we were at home,
without any invitations,
no family cheer,
just us alone, year after year.

Joy Found Me Dancing

Joy didn't knock, she crashed right in,
barefoot, wild, with a crooked grin.
She didn't ask if I was okay,
she pulled me out to dance anyway.

She spun me fast on tired toes,
through every ache my body knows.
She laughed at pain, then kissed my skin,
and dared the light to flood back in.

She traced the scars I used to hide,
then kissed them soft with arms spread wide.
"You've earned your joy," she said, "don't wait—
the world can ache, and still be great."

I threw my shame into the sky,
let go of all the reasons why.
I danced for me, I danced for her—
the child who lived through all that blur.

No mirror needed, no one's praise,
just air and sky and sunlit days.
Joy found me when I dropped the mask,
and showed the world my truest laugh.

Hooves. A Love Story

You called me The Devil
I disagreed
that made you smile
as you do
before crying too
as you do
would The Devil do this?
I said, kissing your cheek yes,
he would you said
and he would leave me too
did you say something else?
I wouldn't have heard anyway
over the noise of my hooves
on your parquet floor

A Father's Love That Endures

He was the kindest soul I knew,
a stepdad's love, so warm and true.

When I couldn't sleep in the middle of the night,
my mother's response was often simple— "just go to sleep."
but my stepdad's care went beyond words.

He'd come to my room, gently stroke and massage my hair,
offering comfort and warmth, showing how much he truly cared.

His kindness extended beyond those quiet nights,
to simple joys like suggesting trips to McDonald's or KFC,
creating moments just for us, filled with love and care.

I often turned him down, not fully aware,
Now I regret those times I said "no,"
not truly appreciating the love he wanted to share.

He was the sweetest,
even when his kindness wasn't always acknowledged.

Though he didn't always receive the response he deserved,
he gave us his heart and grace.

I'm thankful for the times we had,
for a loving stepdad who brought joy into my life.

Though we don't see each other face-to-face now,
and it's not the same as being together in person,
our bond remains strong and meaningful.

Forever grateful for the love he gives,
for the moments we continue to share.

In my heart, his kindness endures,
a treasured connection that continues to grow.

Moved On

A new beginning,
a new dawn,
the birds are chirping all day long.

Arise early the crack of dawn,
plan new things,
and get things done.

Catch up with life,
to where i want to be,
a list before i get too old,
this is my last chance,
to make life more minimal,
and to be at peace,
inner serenity and calm,
that's how life should be.

Erase the madness of younger years.
You're not building an empire because there is only you,
What would be the purpose?
To stress yourself through and through,
none I shout!
There is only you!

Be mindful of the tasks,
be mindful of your use of time,
don't overload,
make everything light and simple as you grow with time.

Missed moments

In the family's circle, I stood apart,
a distant echo in my heart.

Moments missed as I grew tall,
their lives unfolded while I stood alone.

In quiet spaces, I felt unknown.

Uncles, aunts, cousins, nieces, and nephews unseen,
in dreams, I wondered where'd they'd been at twelve,
I joined their world anew,
yet felt the roots i never knew.

Their stories, laughter, lives entwined,
left a longing heart behind.

At twelve, the world came rushing in,
but with lost time, where should I begin?

Rekindled Bonds

Years of silence, then a burst,
at twelve, a door swung open wide,
my mother's kin back by her side.

Accepted now, as she was no longer tied
to the stepdad who once was there.

A family lost and then regained,
the shock of love both sweet and pained.

Faces familiar yet so strange,
a life transformed, a sudden change.

They weren't as I'd imagined, not so humble,
a life i struggled to understand and stumble.

Yet in their company, I felt the light,
the joy was real, the moments bright,
yet the past remained within my sight.

Surreal the change, a dream come true,
in laughter's flood, my blood I knew.

Yet in the sparkle, shadows lay,
a family flawed in their own way.

Still, in my heart, a grateful song,
for family found where I belong.

But in my heart, a wish for you,
stepdad, to see this life unfold,
to share the joy that we hold.

Taunts

Throat against the dark I know
The smells terror I fumble for
The light in the shadows on
The wall faces of closed taunts
Dances your melancholy
Midsummer gaze smiles behind

My soul was dripping
When you touch the story
Of my bare skin since I have
Search for true dew on my lips

Ascea

The blue nuances of the sea are amber for the soul in the
first kiss softness of a beating heart running wild
in the dream catcher horizon and the bay is a droplet
from the beginning of an adventure silhouetted by hands even I
would want to taste

Lost until wrinkles and grey hair hold court smiling in the middle of
November November November and perhaps pour coffee
forget the milk and with slightly shaking hands
burn my tongue a little because I'm somewhere in the middle
of the inner blue of the bay where the mountains understand
my unfolding in the low flight of the birds from the heat of the
balcony

On the skin and the red layers of evening twilight are endless in
the sunset.

The Friend Who Wasn't

You were my one and only friend,
in a world that judged, that would not bend.
Others would laugh, would point and sneer,
not knowing the pain, not knowing the fear.

They mocked my weight, my body, my face,
but they didn't see the hurt in its place.
They didn't know the battles I fought,
the reasons i struggled, the battles i caught.

When I first met you, I thought you were bright,
a shining star, a guiding light.
But as time passed, I saw the cracks,
you weren't all that—just lies and acts.

I chose to stay at your house, night after night,
happy to starve, to shrink from sight.
A can of meatballs for dinner some days,
because that's all you had—at least i ate.

School was my refuge, my place to breathe,
an escape from home, a chance to be free.
But even there, I was pushed aside,
invisible, broken, with nowhere to hide.

But you, you were there, or so I thought,
we laughed together, but those laughs were bought.
I trusted you, with every piece of me,
but now i see you weren't who you claimed to be.

You laughed at my pain, not with me,
took my insecurities and made them a decree.

When I needed a friend to lift me high,
you watched me fall, didn't ask why.

You saw me hurt, yet took from my heart,
fed off my weakness, tore me apart.
I thought you were different, that you understood,
but you were just another hurt, misunderstood.

You made me sleep on that cold, small bed,
while you took the warmth and left me for dead.
The friendship I thought we had, so true,
was just a game to you, nothing new.

I needed someone who would stand by my side,
who wouldn't laugh when i cried.
But instead, you took advantage, time after time,
as i searched for solace, hoping for a sign.

You weren't my friend—not in the way I thought,
just someone who took what you never sought.
You saw my struggles, but turned them to jest,
a "friend" who never cared about what was best.

Now I see clearly, though it took some time,
the love i sought was never really mine.
You fed on my weakness, my quiet despair,
and i was just a fool, thinking you cared.

But look at me now, a changed woman indeed,
stronger, wiser, no longer in need.
The weight you mocked?
Gone without trace,
and now i shine with beauty and grace.

All your insults, the things you would say,
were just your insecurities thrown my way.
I carried your burdens, believed every lie,
but now i stand tall, holding my sky.

I don't need your laugh, I don't need your lie,
I'm stronger now, no longer asking why.
I walked through the storms, through the ridicule and hate,
and I'll leave behind that toxic weight.

You were never the friend I needed to be,
but I've learned to be my own company.
And though the scars still linger, they don't define,
I've found my strength, and i'll be just fine.

In Pursuit

In my pursuit of being a winner
I'm always burning the dinner
As I work to win a prize
It doesn't matter what's the size
The family just gets thinner.

Two Brains, One Battle From the Body of a Survivor

I carried weight like armour — thick, unmissed,
years inside a body the world dismissed.
"Morbidly obese," they said with cold eyes,
as if i didn't know the shape of my own size.

But they never saw my fatty brain,
always hungry. always in pain.
Food was comfort, food was friend,
food filled the silence i couldn't defend.

I binged when I broke, when sadness would rise,
when loneliness pressed beneath swollen thighs.
Every bite was a scream I couldn't say,
every craving begged the hurt to go away.

And then—
The weight fell. Fast. Sharp. Unrelenting.
My body shrank, but my mind kept inventing.
I'd said "I'm not hungry" so many times,
My brain rewired in subtle rhymes.

Now I have what I call an "anorexia mind,"
where eating feels selfish, indulgent, unkind.
Where I flinch at fullness, where less feels like peace,
where I fear the return of my former disease.

It's quiet now — too quiet some days.
No bingeing, no comfort, no emotional haze.
But freedom? No, not quite that yet.
Just different rules, same heavy debt.

From obese to "thin," the world claps loud —
but they don't see the fear I'm wrapped around.
Because healing isn't just what you weigh,
it's the thoughts you carry every day.

I long for a brain that doesn't swing
from devour everything to deny everything.
A brain that trusts, that nourishes deep,
that lets me feel, lets me eat, lets me sleep.

Because I survived both sides of this war —
and I deserve a life that's something more.
Not a body to fear. Not a mind to fight.
but peace — in the mirror, in appetite, in night.

Little by Little

I don't rush this healing now,
I've learned to go slow, and still allow.
No finish line, no race to run—
just soft hellos to who I've become.

I speak to me with kinder words,
not ones that sting or go unheard.
I touch my heart like fragile glass,
and let the heavy moments pass.

I hold my fears with open hands,
no need to fight what still demands.
I let the tears fall when they may,
then gently wipe the rest away.

I dress in clothes that make me glow,
and smile at mirrors once feared so.
I thank my legs for getting through,
my arms for all they've carried too.

I don't need perfect to feel whole,
I just need space to feed my soul.
And little by little, breath by breath,
I come back home to me from death.

Getting up in the Morning

Tick tock alarm clock
Sitting by my head
Tock tick feeling sick
Ring in to say I'm dead
Take a pill, lie still
Alarm goes, throw on clothes
Cup of tea does revive
Now I feel alive
Go to work or stay away?
Probably the only decision I need to make today.

I Am Not What Happened

I am not the hands that hurt,
not the silence, not the dirt.
Not the names they threw like knives,
not the years that dimmed my life.

I am not the fear they fed,
not the weight of words I've said.
Not the nights I shook with shame,
not the echoes of their name.

I am breath and beating heart,
a soul they tried to tear apart.
But here I stand, and here I speak—
a voice that rose when I was weak.

I am thunder, I am flame,
I've stitched my wounds, reclaimed my name.
I built a life from ruins, bare,
and found my power buried there.

So let them whisper, let them lie—
they couldn't kill the will to try.
I'm not their past, their hate, their sin—
I'm everything they couldn't win.

I Fell Again

I fell again—don't ask me how,
just know I'm standing taller now.
The dark still knows the shape I make,
but it can't hold what it can't break.

I slipped on grief, I tripped on shame,
old ghosts still whispering my name.
The past came knocking like it knew
just when to flood my sky with blue.

But falling isn't where I stay—
I cry, I shake, I find my way.
I speak the truth through trembling lips:
this healing life is not a script.

There's no clean line, no final scene,
just messy steps in spaces between.
Some days I shine, some days I ache,
but every breath is one I take.

So judge me not for how I fall—
applaud the fact I rise at all.
I carry scars, but not regret.
I'm healing still. I'm not done yet.

Let It Pass

It's okay to be broken, to not feel whole,
to carry the weight deep in your soul.
Don't let their words drag you down—
you're not their storm, you're not their frown.

My therapist says, when they come with rage,
it's their own hurt they're trying to wage.
They hold out their pain, wrapped as a gift—
but you don't have to carry that rift.

Refuse the load, just walk away—
their anger is theirs, let them find their way.
You don't need to fix what they won't face,
you deserve peace, not their displaced grace.

If you need to cry, let the tears fall,
there's strength in the cracks, in feeling it all.
Breathe through the ache, the throb, the sting—
even the darkest nights change into spring.

These moments will pass, I swear they will,
the chaos will quiet, the world will still.
Hold on, be gentle, take it slow—
you're healing, you're growing, you're letting go.

The Alarm Clock – I

The Alarm clock bell is ringing
and the world comes crushing in
chasing all my dreams away
another day begins
Another day of serving time on the 9-5
another life time stole away by the daily grind
every day is just the same
it's the same each week
working like slaves to make ends meet
if I could, I know I would escape from this RR.

A Pocketful of Paradise.

I picked a pinch of golden sand,
and popped it in my pocket,
I grabbed a bunch of anecdotes,
my heart soared like a rocket.

I added a cube of mouldy cheese,
some apple, and a biscuit.

Then I threw in a field mouse,
was silly, but i risked it.

I caught hold of the sunshine,
added it with care.

Then chucked in some morning kisses,
and a single lock of hair.

Next I threw in laughter,
that came straight from my belly.

The kind that makes your ribs hurt,
and your legs turn into jelly.

A simple little daisy chain,
along with an ear of corn.

That silly, tatty teddy,
I've had since i was born.

Finally I added my garden,
and the wishing well.

The favourite words my husband says,
and that's I love you shell.

Now I've a pocketful of Paradise,
that no one else can see,
concealed about my person,
It means everything to me!!

What if...

What if bees only hum,
because they do not know the words,
or slugs are homeless snails,
that thought is so absurd.

What if patients,
have no patience,
and song birds
can not sing,
and starter motors didn't start,

The stupid bloody thing.
what if cheetahs were not cheaters,
and ladybirds were male,
or the yacht was just a boat,
without it's big white sail.

What if hatred turned to love,
all captives were set free,
a world of empathy and compassion,
joy and harmony.

What if leaders throughout this planet,
worked together for greater good,
no war and power struggles,
no one misunderstood.

I'm Worthy, I'm Enough.

In the mirror there's my reflection,
not how it used to be,
my face vaguely familiar,
but is it really me.

My eyes they seemed so lifeless,
no brightness like before,
the memories have dulled them,
since my mind was sent to war.

I survived but left with mental scars,
by all who did me wrong,
but then i took to writing,
surprisingly i grew strong.

Turmoil, stress and anxiety,
was deep inside of me,
but poems and free writing,
finally set me free.

So I wear my scars like tiger stripes,
and show myself compassion,
because this kind of expressive love,
won't ever go out of fashion.

From now on I'll remind myself,
that when my life gets tough,
I have already survived these storms before,
I'm worthy, I am enough.

Sweet Baby

Oooh baby, you're so sweet!
I get this funny feeling every time that we meet
the air starts crackling with electricity
every time you move your body up close to me
my heart starts pounding I struggle to breath.
I break into a sweat and go weak at the knees
I'm not quite sure what is happening to me
I guess it's a reaction to your chemistry
I just can't get you off my mind
you got me thinking what if you were mine
you got me thinking of you all the time.

Nothing To See Here

...Meanwhile, in a week that has seen the hottest average global temperature ever recorded on Tuesday, surpassing the previous record set on Monday (crisis, what crisis?)...

Present your spreadsheets to the wind.
Boast those quarterlies to the ocean.
Forecast dividends yet to come
Before this planet's baking sun.
   Move along there dear,
   Nothing for you to see back here.

I viewed my basket
And after one final mouse click,
My brand new shades were winging their way.
And when they arrive the very next day,
They're guaranteed to illicit
The same happiness explicit,
On the faces
 Of those models
   And the model friends who visit them.
It's daunting,
But all I need do
Is keep buying
The same stuff as they're wearing,
And flaunting and trying,
To make every precious pound it takes,
But it's worth it.
Yeah, I'm worth it,
Just like them.
I'm only trying to be happy,
Just as happy,
Just like them.

Present your spreadsheets to the wind.
Boast those quarterlies to the ocean.
Forecast dividends yet to come

Before this planet's baking sun.
> *Move along there dear,*
> *Nothing for you to see back here.*

She's also viewing her basket
And after putting a few things back,
She can just about afford
What's on the tiller's touch screen pad.
Her day isn't long under way
And now sat on the bus to the factory,
She gazes back in the direction of her flat,
Then down to the backpack
Perched on her lap,
And then to her ripening, raspberry blisters.
Same town,
　Same choices,
　　Same life as her sisters.
The petrochemical quilt
All but filters
Out the sun.
From the high-rise of the sweatshops
Beyond the low-rise squalor,
Where every piece
Of essential tat's journey begun.

Seldom complains;
Her family moved in from the plains;
　Four failed crops
　　From poor, ailed rains,
Then the four years, came all at once,
Washed the whole valley
And its topsoil down the drains.
If she puts in a hundred hours,
She just about retains
Around three dollars a week for her pains.
For the never satisfied appetite
Of another world remains.
Where the effects of a man made crisis
Are maybe a few degrees here and there,

And some flooding or some fires.
   Yeah, there was something on the news
   ...Who cares.

Present your spreadsheets to the wind.
Boast those quarterlies to the ocean.
Forecast dividends yet to come
Before this planet's baking sun.
   Move along there dear,
   Nothing for you to see back here.

On An Ancient Face Is Inscribed

On an ancient face is inscribed
Lines of age and experience.
Which tells tales.
A closer look reveals ancient beauty now and then.
What splendour is there?
How many hearts broken?
Hopes destroyed and advances rebuffed?
We didn't talk
And I couldn't ask if that apparent sereneness
was contentment or resignation.
The fatal stance of being beyond the last dance.
The unseeing stare while still alive.
And soon death's resigned farewell.

Strings Attached

From the burial mound above Bostraze
You can see both coasts;
Greeb Point jutting out near Morvah,
Around to Pendeen Watch, then on to the nose
Of Cape Cornwall on the North.
And then from the mouth
Of Gwennap Head beyond Polgigga,
Along to Porthcurno on the South.

The distant horizon;
Squinting into the glinting,
Semantic Atlantic.
Lost,
In examining the imagining of a neolithic settlement...
Drawn
Into its bedrock, to unlock
Some perspective, reflective
Of why this ancient place was deemed
Sanctified,
Sacred.

Lengthy focal points seem to lend themselves
To peering into near futures,
Or rearward, to the befores.
The far distance displays a haze of helpful absence,
With ample space to grace
And trace with wonder.
Up close and under
The nose, less light.
No surprises up close, right?

But it was a Stonechat that made me look,
Tumbling out of its cloudless height like a stringless kite,
To flit between the rich heathers of iris, lilac and violet,
And the freshly glossed gorse of gold, canary and pineapple.

Then it was the steady humming,
Like a strings section warming up.
Bees!
Hundreds ...no, thousands of bees!
Heads down, eyes forward.
This, their work.

Feverishly gathering nectar.
Drawn by what; Smell? ...Colour? ...Shape?
A slave to their unfettered senses.
Driven by pure instinct.

Yet inadvertently, these little creatures are almost solely responsible for the
Intricate tapestry scrunched around,
To comfort this elderly, hunched, cold ground,
Like a shawl found
For its bony limbs.
Without the preoccupied bees this exposed place would be left to shiver.
With no colour,
And little sound.

   I caught myself attempting
   To serve up a generous slice
   Of sage advice
   Last week,
   To a more sleek
   Next generation,
   Lower emission,
   Sharper edition,
   Newer version.
   Though I had this suspicion,
   I could be missing,
   Some immediate ingredient...
   Still, undeterred,
   I presented my case
   And delivered earnest portions
   Of serious cautions (for me),
   Of this cub's pathway,
   But only ever halfway to see.

Because when there are
Strings attached,
Sometimes the strings are all I see.
Those conditional ties,
That even when I squint,
My focus flicks back to that
Troublesome, small-print.

But how many warnings
Might have been given to those regaining their feet,
Getting back up
To move forward,
Those trip hazards! (not ideal, never neat).
Had a strong word with my accessible,
If sceptical self;
Who was I to stand in the way of fate
Let alone love, shared in equal portions.
Different cautions but essentially the same.
When the very things warned of,
Could ultimately bring such fulfilment, such joy for them.
Both manna and purpose
For a journey,
Again.

I watched as the bees,
Carrying on in some obsessive, irrational, inexplicable, instinctive urge,
Whilst accidentally ferrying pollen from flower to flower.
A mere side-effect;
A beautiful, incidental by-product
To be appreciated only from the far distance
From the thing under their very noses;
The job of work
To which their tiny hearts were true,
And of the thing they somehow felt,
That they simply
Had to do.

We Are Dust

We are dust,
made and born
We are dust,
naked, forlorn

We are dust,
called mankind
We are dust,
ties that bind

We are dust,
in life and death
We are dust,
till our last breath

We are dust,
people mourn
We are dust,
earth reborn

We are dust,
we are dust,
we
Are
Dust…

Interesting & Possible

Ignorant people are
unable to learn and unwilling
and therefore will never understand
true knowledge
and will continue to treat things
with fear and selfish emotions
and will remain forever lost and depressed
stuck in an unending loop.

Legacy

She was quite direct this time,
And seemed less concerned it might hurt.
Said I'm not my new haircut
And not this new season's tee-shirt.
And as for my labels,
And as for my slogans and words;
They are nothing but dust
In the down of the feathers of birds.

Invading my dreams she then
Lectured me like a true friend.
Said I'm not the result,
And I'm not how my story will end.
In the hands of all others,
My voice could be mute as a mime.
It's the choices I make that define
What I am for all time.

She held out her hand, it was steady,
My fingers found hers.
Her voice knew my fear,
But her words formed the sweetest of verse.
She said, "love is painful".
I followed her lips as she talked,
"You will be your motives,
 You will be the path that you walked".

For a moment an echo
Of Sunday school came into view.
Something about serpents, of Adam,
And his free will too.
But then just as quickly it faded
And all I could see,
Was the core of an apple,
And the blessings and curse of a tree.

She might come again,
I don't know, but I'll wait each new moon.
Cos I may need reminding,
I might need some comforting soon.

If awareness is key,
Then the child in me is afraid,
That my legacy won't be much more
Than the choices I made.

My legacy won't be much more
Than the choices I made...

Natural Love

Like springs making streams
Into rivers that run to the sea
Is like the force the force that's in creation
That led my heart to thee.
And if I had a harmonic voice
My love for you I'd sing
And if I could have my choice
A black rose to you I'd bring.
And though rough fresh diamond
Doesn't sparkle when first of all it's found
What is pure and true in beauty
Is Love's mystery most profound.

Bodmin Moor

Roughtor, Brown Willy,
Dozmary Pool,
a landscape wild, and wonderful

With Weathered rocks,
bent over trees,
both ravaged by the winds and breeze

There's talk of beasts,
The Excalibur story,
let's not forget the Bodmin Moor Pony

King Arthur's Hall
Trevethy Quot
The Pipers and the Hurlers

With standing stones,
and ancient sites
Inhabited through the ages

Cornwall, my Cornwall
Forever you are proud.
Bodmin Moor, ethereal,
it's mist is her shroud

She rises from the valleys,
She rises from the cliffs,
The guardian of Cornwall,
In command of her precious gifts.

True, Authentic Self

Be your true, authentic self,
do what you desire.
Be your true, authentic self,
nothing else really matters.

Be your true authentic self,
you have your own life's mission.
Be your true, authentic self,
ignore the news and politicians.

Be your true, authentic self,
peel back the layers of doubt.
Be your true, authentic self,
take a moment, scream and shout.

Be your true, authentic self,
time to grow and time to heal.
Be your true, authentic self,
for only you know how you feel.

Be your true, authentic self,
burn the image you were before.
Be your true, authentic self,
life really is too short.

Be your true, authentic self,
time to rise up from the ashes.
Be your true authentic self,
nothing else really matters.

Woke

Being woke is a term
certain people see as negative,
but to me it is the opposite,
being woke is a positive,

The definition states
that woke means the following:
    "being aware and attentive
    to important facts and issues,
    especially those related
    to race and social justice."

If that's the definition,
then being woke is not a slur,
it proves that you are human
it proves that you care

In a world full of hate
being woke is what will save us
for I'd rather be woke
than some hateful, bigot

Being woke is a term
certain people see as negative,
But I's time that we changed
this divisive narrative,

The people need to rise,
The earth needs to quake,
As well as being woke, let's be awake!!

Belief

Did you hear that David's moved on?
So we're not in touch like we used to be,
actually hardly ever, actually not at all, but that's him,
as long as he's happy, he would have been in touch,
I'm sure, if he wasn't.

I've moved on too, living at the other end of town-
I miss the old house but David used to deal with everything,
that was his way.
I didn't even know when it was recycling, that was his thing.

Totally different we were, I'm sure that's why we got on so well.
Age didn't come into it, although I always recognised
there'd be a future without him, I'm not daft.

And it worked out well enough.
I have a new life for sure, but mostly I'm doing well,
and that's all you want out of life isn't it?

Not the highs and the lows, you just want your life to be o.k.
And that's fine by me.

Although of course I do miss him.

An Island Home Of Light

An island of light beckons
across the sea of forgetfulness.
Pain, worry, despair,

sink below its waters,
land amongst the stones of sadness,
rocks of regret.

Towards the sunset of our life
comes a dawning of delight,
a casting off from shores of sorrow,

leaving slippery seaweed of surrender,
and facing acceptance,
love and light.

Indra's Net

I step unknowingly into Indra's net, a web of knowing,
an emptiness of which I was unaware,
but which suddenly became filled
with random, delightful connections.

    I over brim with sunlight
        I am warmed by its rays
            I am revived, refreshed
                  by a touch
                      by a word
                          by a conversation
One after another,   these jewels come,
sending tingles of light,   reflecting brightness.

I note that there are five that speak my voice,
they in turn may realise their infinite power
but do not have my voice,
may only feel a transient lightness in their sorrow.

It seemed a humble place, a simple time,
but this powerful net holds me wrapped
in its arms and bids me return,
calm in my knowing, I leave.

Today, Without Warning, I Enter The Lion's Den

It started with the voice-
Brows furrowed
I want to talk to you- and I want you to listen-
It's serious.

The door swung open
He held the latch
Prodded me with a fingered word
Pushed me forwards

Danger lurked
I kept quiet
Stared into that face
The lion I knew yesterday

Shook its mane
I felt its menace.
The hair and saliva of its fear
Flicked my face

But I lowered my eyes
And stepped backwards
Not today
Not today.

Gaza Haiku

Alone in Gaza
a child looks
for a parent
rubble in Gaza

Your Song Reaches The Laughing Leaves

Your song reaches the laughing leaves
on the smallest tree.
Loud and proud you strut,
amongst the ivy and cheery dandelions.
Flick you tail, as we glimpse your leaving.

High up in the mountains your song
reaches prayer flags fluttering,
carries your words to the highest in that land.
Your song reaches across air waves, made celestial
Your song travels over time.

Your song is learned from birth
Rocked in the motherland of womanhood
Soothed in the saying of whispers, taken from the music of water
The layering love of maternity,
The feeding comfort and safety.

Our song will carry through lifetimes;
 mingle with nature and purpose,
strengthen through bonds of resilience,
hold with the prayers of the world,
and listen to the wisdom of ancestors.

Trapped

It was one of those days,
when I watched helplessly
as nature continued its cruel journey.

It was already too late.
The worldly body was already ensnared,
its flights of fancy failed.

The freedom to fly and flourish, over.
The short steps towards the end, inescapable.
The silk web of silence.

Caught, trapped
and slowly wrapped,
its beautiful earthly body.

A body designed to support and
step from garden to garden,
flower to flower.

Support, supply and simply bee.
And now it was wrapped
and bound in spider's silk.

And silent.
It's end complete.

The Well of St Morwenna

Way down the cliff edge
There doth lye a well
Not far from Heaven, but not far from hell
To Venture there tis a pilgrim's peril
Especially when the sea's a raging turmoil
And Leviathan and Behemoth
Endlessly toil.

Morwenna she came from across the sea
From Cymru Lands to Kernow's shore
A daughter of the Celtic badger
To instruct in the ways of the Lord
The not long converted Saxon.

When labouring font stone up yon treacherous cliff
All cause for the church foundation
She paused for breath, gave thanks and blessed
The Lord of all creation.

She picked up stone resuming Quest
And where stone did rest on ground so blessed
It wept its soul's libation.
And pilgrim did venture from far and near
To be touched by the water
So pure, so clear
A place that Morwenna in her heart held so dear

The years passed by
And Morwenna went crying
Down to the well she knew the Lord's calling
And in her brother Nectan's arms
Her righteous soul did pass
And the sight she beheld the last
Through her tear blurred sight
Her nature Cymru's distant shores
Across the stormy sea

cont.

Way down the cliff edge
There doth lye a well
Not far from Heaven, but not far from hell
To Venture there tis a pilgrim's peril
Especially when the sea's a raging turmoil
And Leviathon and Behmoth
Endlessly toil.

The Falling Leaves Of Autumn

The wind blows harsh and shakes the tress
Then the leaves fall down on a gentle breeze
They all fall down onto the floor
A rainbow myriad of colour
And shapes galore
A spider's web shimmers in the morning's dew
Then a big fat man sweeps them up
Into a pile and then burns them up
There are no more leaves anymore
Until next year then there will be more

written at age 9

The Passing Of The Wind: AKA The Prezident Erected

The president elected couldn't get a grip
And from his orange big fat greasy bum
The trump it didn't half rip!
It caused a slip that caused a slick
That made a smell so vile and sick
And to say the least that all's not well
It smelted like it came from the bowels of hell.
And he says from his mouth al hell will be released
For he doesn't want Palestinians to live in love and peace.
The president elected is a convicted felon
That likes to rule with claws like talon
What kind of people vote for such a farce
A man that perpetually blusters gas from his mouth and arse.
Though hand on in there, can't you see
There's a ray of hope for humanity
It's really rather simple and very clear to me
The man produces so much gas
From now on it should be free.

United States of Israel

Oh, what happened to America
land of the free, and so on.
Bible belted land, yet black Christians be told
KKK and the bible belt –
Christians be divided in to colours and class.

Christian disunity – thus cattle
the country, yet the wolves in
sheeps clothes that shepherd the flock
worship the green king
their temple, known as the wall in the street,

God only knows what is happening
in the clandestine world of America
the slaves, the first nation,
they're all shifted and stifled
to make way for the bible belt with bible slaves.
And the Capitol is ruled by the green king worshipers
with an eye in the pyramid

What is happening in the clandestine America
collusion and ills, dancing Mo
Sads in the twin's of tower collapse,
Benjamin in the senate, hail
with foreign aid, to un-Palestine
and the apartheid to reign supreme

The sheeps sleep in America just be keeps
The brains are ruling with the green king
from the middle of the east
Media keeps the country sweet
and injects them the vaccine they need
to keep them down, so they syphon out of
America to fund the capitol in the new
Je-r-us-
a- American's
l- lives
e- equate
m- minuscule

To A Lost Wild Beauty.

Not knowing what I saw

I glimpsed

The strangely coiled whiteness

        of

           Your tiny nasal concha,

As delicate as lace, a miracle of spiralled bone.

Underneath the Asphodel,

      I found your shapely skull, your ribs, your spine,

Curled as if in sleep amid your bleached and reflexed limbs

        That danced for joy upon this sun-dried land of mine

Throughout your few short summers

When

You made this place your own.

I fondly watched you gallivant,

    Play silly

      And,

        Play dead,

Only to spring and dance again as if you meant to please…

The twilight birds have left this hour to me and,
To the Dead.
Night stumbles in relentlessly across each troubled wave.
I see once more the flicker of your green eyes in the moon
And smell your feral fur in fancy
As you sneak anew into my once-strong arms
To lick the tears softly from my cheek
While in my head
Dishonestly I disallow my own awaiting grave.

Once Upon A Time....

A princess is in a despair
A princess is looking for a prince
An expectation from the princess is quite a lot to see
A prince is expecting a princess to follow his golden rules
A golden rules has been arranged for the princess to follow
once they start to live together in a huge castle

A castle is made up of gold and marbles
Indeed a beautiful castle you could ever imagine
All well built up in a modern time with a highly quality furniture
A furniture are all made up of wood and silk
Indeed very expensive

So do prince and princess are expecting
 a high gross incomes once living together
Nothing can break that
A very strong relationship in the Royal family
Not even a person can break that easily

Self Knowledge

When temporarily destroyed
By guilt, despair, or loneliness
We can no longer bear our days,
Listen for the voices
That echo down the years,
Let them explain the origin
Of our loves, antipathies and fears,
Recognise the sense of oneness
With those from far-off lands,
Meeting not as strangers, but familiars,
As places remembered yet unseen.
Discovering our ancestors,
By knowing them, ourselves,
Interpreting the music
We may understand the song.

Tango Dream

The music beckons
Weaves its spell,
Eyes meet and smile
Hands touch, ignite
As palms explore,
Strong arms enfold
Heart against heart
We sway, limbs move
You lead, I follow
The world retreats,
We are aware
Only of each other
Slowly we dance as one
The dance of love and death
Our joys, our sorrow

Remembered passion.

Once Upon A Time – Empty House

There is a house which has been found empty
An abandoned house all by itself
In the middle of nowhere to be seen

We were wondering who was the owner of an empty house
As we approached to have a closer look
To our horror
We found a lot of rats!

Indeed.... Lots of rats are looking for cheese
Yes those rats can smell CHEEESSSEEE!
All they want is to eat the delicious cheese
They sniff and follow the smell of cheese

There is also a blood to be found at the empty house
Quite SCARILY I got to say
We ever wondering where does the blood comes from
Oh my lord!
We found the blood that came from the death body underneath the basement
Oh my lord! It's smell so AWFUL!

We even call the police
SIREN....SIREN.....SIREN
Police are on their way
Investigation are taking place
Found the murderer
Murderer are arrested and locked up in the cell

Taking time to clear the empty house
Hand it over to the new owner of the house
Renovation and makeover is all needed
To make the house look beautiful with new family moving in shortly

A happy family live in there with a happy ending

Come with Me

Come walk with me
Through flowers
The swaying grass
In the wind
Come dance with me
On sun-warm sand,
Swim in the Shimmering sea
Come lie with me
Dream by my side
Asleep in the Mellow hay
Come ride with me
To the edge of the sun
Where splintered Shadows play,
And the rising amber
Or our desire
Hallows the summer's day
Come into me
On wings of light
As the spindrift clouds Sail by,
And the tears in my eyes
Will tell you
Dying is in goodbye.

Don't Buy Me Flowers

Don't buy me flowers .
when the world
one day awakens with out me
and the sunrise fills the sky
with a beautiful glow of hope .
as the stars do wishes
and the moon with dreams .
no longer dark clouds
rain sleet hail or snow
shall ever fall upon my bear skin .

No longer will Luna cast my shadow
...The dark days
those thunderstorms
have now gone .
no longer do I carry this heavy load
...The wars I was so tired of
I thought would never end...is over ...
the silence of my voice
no longer echoes in the house..
don't cry for me
because I am now free..

From the mental torment
that crippled and distorted me
Don't buy me flowers.
plant seeds of peace and love
understanding wisdom
sow seeds of honesty
 be firm but always be kind...
find strength within
you will need it on your journey
it can sometimes wear you thin
don't buy me flowers
you never did when I was around
So put your money in your pocket

and save yourself a pound...
don't cry for me
be happy for me
as I am now free
of the things I never let you see.

The things that taunted me .
Don't buy me flowers
they will be left to rot in a cheesy pot
until the next time
you waste your money
and replace the last lot ...
Sprinkle some of my ashes
in the beautiful sea
remember good times
remember me .
sprinkle some of me
underneath a nice strong tree
in the valley...
may be sometimes
you could come and
watch the sun go down with me

Poets

We are the dreamers of each others dreams,
scribes whose unsung words are heard
by those with hearts to understand,
who soar with our imagining.

Hear the music behind the words
whisper poetry to prose,
attempt to catch the gossamer
severed from the wing.

Music

Music is so powerful
I don't think we fully understand
it can bring people together
united as we stand ..

A beautiful symphony
that sings to me
every note pulls on my strings
a warm vibration to sooth the mind
leave the world of madness behind.. .. .

so dance or just tap your feet to the Rhythm
to the beat
lose yourself
set yourself free
come on and dance
feel the good vibrations
feel free ....

move your feet
feel that beet .
there will always be a melody
that reminds you of a time
a day
 a place
a person
it's true
that's the power of what music can do .

the right tune
the right song
can have you humming all day .
silly irritating worm...
music can make your heart sink
and fade to your feet
it touches something

much deeper than your soul
something out of our control
a vibration that grips
manipulate your emotions .
there will forever be a song .
for the time
lines in our chapters .
memory's from a song will
always live on
they sit deep inside
our hippocampus
mind I think that's what you'll find...

music is a key
you can not see
but it can unlock a memory
it is my medication
it really does have a vibration
for every occasion
it can set a mood
feed your soul
with musical food

Waiting For The Summer

I'm waiting for the summer
When I can discard these winter blues
To feel the sunshine upon my face
To see the roses in the maze

I'm waiting for the summer
To see the smiles on peoples faces
To smell the perfume of the roses
In the garden

I'm waiting for the summer
And the days full of sunshine
And the sound of birdsong
As they fly by in a azure blue sky

I'm waiting for the summer
When artists take up their easels
To paint the glory of it all
In the colours of the rainbow

I'm just sat here
Patiently
Waiting
For the summer

Lost And Found

I felt like I'd just swallowed sunshine'
She said
When she met
The person she'd been searching for
All her life

The son she'd given up
When she had no choice
When she was so young
Now re-united
With the son she'd lost

Never too late
To search
For lost love
To be re-united
In the sunshine of love

Always Know that I Still Matter

As a child they called her odd,
a bit strange.

Usually when in trouble,
misunderstanding the words they say.

Translating the language heard,
in a very different way.

Inquisitive and curious,
discovering a way to cope,
hiding within herself,
watching others play.

So talented they barked at her one day,
it's just her way of communicating,
as they watched her brushes sway.

Masterpieces produced at the end of each day,
from the girl they called a mischief in a melancholy way.

The Love That Grows

He walked on the street,
with his head looking down.

Not seeing the girl,
who saw him in a crown.

He said hello,
all shy.

Her heart soared so high.
they started talking,
which led to walking.

As things progressed,
they built a nest.

The years went by,
the love was high.

Then that day arrived,
when one flew to the sky.

The other was left,
by that graveside.

Memories visited,
smiles would arise.

Remembering the beauty,
of those twinkling eyes.

A Lonely Child With Skies Of Blue

When he left:
a father's absence at nine years old,
my world fell apart,
my stepdad gone, leaving a void in my heart.

He was my guide, a bond so strong,
in his absence, I felt I didn't belong.

The love I knew was now out of sight,
leaving me to face the lonely night.

In empty spaces, echoes remained,
of laughter, love, and memories ingrained.

If I Hurry Up The Hill

My body since you died
Is crumbling

Various diseases, infections,
Pains and torments

I stopped wanting to die
But now It seems more likely

And before that endless tries
To be well
Things to swallow
Procedures
Regimes
Fear of decay and pain

If I hurry up the hill
Home from the doctor

Could my heart fail?
Instant death

Like my mother's friend
Went upstairs to get a hat
Fell down
I don't mind that.

Run Melania Run blues

Run Melania Run.
Run Melania Run
Get to the refuge quickly
Spill the beans to the press
Help us to get that Donald
Just what he deserves
Before he does more damage
To our precious world

Run Melania Run
Run Melania Run
You can really help us out
Tell everyone the truth
Of what Trump's all about
Move on to a better life
Than as that so very
Crazy bad man's wife

Run Melania run,
Run Melania run.
We know you can't stand him
We see it in your face
An immigrant yourself
What a bad thing, honey
 To share his money

Run Melania run
Run Melania run
What a price you paid
But you can leave now
You can get aid
Run for safety
Do not be afraid

Run Melanie Run
Run Melanie Run.

Blue sky

To see green leaves against a pure blue sky
is a smile inducing moment and makes my heart fly
the blue without clouds
is a beautiful scene we have waited so long with the rain in between.

I sit on my bench staring into the trees
I see squirrels and birds, butterflies and bees –
playing gently in nature no fear or divide
playing in and out of leaves with the sun on their side.

We are only in May So we hope for more sun
we can start each new day knowing we'll have some fun.
To see green leaves against a pure blue sky
Is the best in the world and makes my heart fly.

Voices in Silence

Here is a poem inspired by the current situation (August 2024) in Bangladesh

In shadows deep, where fears reside,
Students rebellious voice, a nation's pride.

Their words, a beacon, bright and clear,
inspire thousands, dispel the fear.

Silent cries from distant lands,
echo through our hearts, our hands.

Neighbours here, afraid to speak,
Their families' safety, frail and weak.

Independence Day, we loudly cheer,
Yet Bangladeshi hearts, they shed a tear.

It's more than protests in the street,
A revolution's thrum, a heartbeat.

Two hundred souls to heaven soared,
Thousands more behind locked doors.

Teachers stand with students' plight,
Guardians of both mind and life.

To the world, we call for justice grand,
For humanity, extend your hand.

In Bangladesh, let voices ring,
Freedom's song, let courage bring.

Respect to all who bravely fight,
In darkest times, for what is right.

Thank you, heroes, far and near,
For standing tall, for shedding fear.

Lonely Man

Lonely man
With downcast eyes
Walking the winter streets
Shoeless
With ragbound feet
Lonely man
 Unkempt and wild

Hard to imagine
You were a child
Lonely man
What have you become?
How did it happen
To somebody's son?

A Bloody Bangladesh

It took some time, but now they see —
this movement will not fade away.

The students will not leave the streets,
their voices rising day by day.

Now, those in power change their tone, asking,
"What is the alternative?"
But no one plans a storm like this.

Those who rise are the ones who build new paths.
These are not timid children.

They carry knowledge, patience, and conscience.

They hold the power to shape tomorrow,
and In-Sha-Allah, they will lead this nation.

Let no government take anything for granted.

A country is its people — and power must walk hand in hand with
responsibility.

To silence the people is to break the nation.
But to listen, to speak, to work together —
is to build a future that is just and beautiful for all.

For Steve

You asked me too,
Just marry you.

You asked me too,
Just say I do.

My heart was won,
Your eyes,

They shone.
Like twinkling seas,

Kissed by the sun.
I said I do,

And married you.

Now we're stuck together,
Just like glue.

A Cry for Justice

(The poem is dedicated to all those students who have given their lives to save democracy and freedom in July/August 2024)

I cannot believe my eyes and ears!
Please, tell me the terrible clips floating
around social media are from 1971.
The boy recited the poem in a rebellious voice.
I don't know who he is,
but his essence and actions would inspire thousands.

I feel for my fellow Bangladeshis,
unable to express their feelings - even in the UK,
some of my neighbours and friends are terrified—
Afraid to speak, worried for the safety of family back home.
We proudly celebrate Independence Day,
yet Bangladeshi people cannot say how they feel.

This is not just a protest— It is a revolution.
I mourn over 200 deaths, and thousands arrested.
I appreciate all the teachers,
who have joined the protest in support of students.
They have proven they care not just for education,
but for well-being and life itself.

The International Criminal Court must step in
Begin a preliminary examination of crimes against humanity:
Murder, imprisonment, and inhumane acts in Bangladesh.

My respect to you all.

Thank you so much.

Is It Too Late

Your breath cooled the fires
and you created wonders,
gave us personal choice
with slow-won skills
to build a paradise,
your truths diffused
by artists, thinkers, prophets
having failed by our non-caring,
lack of love,
misuse of science,
can we prevent the holocaust, or
are we already sentenced
to the flames of pre-creation,
is humanity to die
in a hell of its own making,
while Satan robed in triumph
rules the cooling ashes?

Self-Respect:

The Path to Being Respected It is a tradition—
or so they believe—
To act so smart, with tricks up their sleeve.
They think they're capable, clever, and bright,
Interesting, intelligent—always right.

Some people delight in making you wait,
Others look down with a smirk full of hate.
If you're needy, they'll gladly extend their hand,
Offering sympathy, as if it were planned.

They wear an attitude, make you feel small,
But what they don't know—it's your spirit that calls.
They don't realize you see through the guise,
Their judgments mean nothing—no surprise.

Why let them underestimate your grace?
Why give them power to dictate your place?
Why let them mock you just to feel grand,
When you can rise strong, with your life in hand?

Don't wait for their favour, don't give them the reins—
Let them feel pleasure, but it's all in vain.
Care for yourself, turn inward, take charge—
Your strength and your will are infinitely large.

And one day they'll see—it's a slap to the face:
You played your own game, at your own pace.
No, they didn't toy with your heart or emotion—
It was you who stirred the deeper commotion.

If Princess Anne

If Princess Anne
or Charlie Chan
got on the bus
without any fuss
with all of us
nobody would notice.

Amazonian Alexa

Alexa, you're just an instrument of Satan
Why you gonna follow me?
Why you gonna analyse and record me?
Judgement day is a dawning
See the sign and warning
The truth it a flowing
Gonna fill the Earth and water fill the sea
It's the fate of all humanity

Said love and peace and community
It's the only way to be naturally
Said all this the computer shit
It's for the fuck wit
Said it only gonna end up a buried in a pit, eh?

The time is coming and I tell you no lie
Babylon in a hell it go fry
They might try and keep on trying
But it founded on a lie and there is no denying
The only truth come from Jah

And like the water cover the sea
It gonna be the truth of humanity
And every eye shall see
Said the day is dawning
Said can you see the sign and the warning?
Babylon falling
Babylon sinking
Can you see the corrupt shit dem a stinking.

The Way I Love My Matty Dread

Fresh and calm like a breeze
Fierce as a hurricane
As refreshing as a spring shower
Wet like October rain

As still as a July ocean
Pure like a mountain spring
As strong as the strongest man
As gentle as a new born babe

As verdant as an oak in June
As bright and clear as the fullest moon
Warm on my face like summer sun
How I love you, Matty mon.

As splendorous as a mountain view
As sparkly as the morning dew
As gracious as the birds that fly
Shining like stars in the night sky

Ever radiant like our love for Jah
Reaching deep and stretching far
Where you go next is where I want to be
I need you here, next to me.

No Answers

Night of endless questions
What purpose in my being?
What future in my death?
The end or a beginning?
Adrift in timeless limbo?
Perhaps a spiritually guided tour
To Heaven or to Hell?
There to exist forever?
But will I never tire?
Will there be no sleeping, waking,
Hunger or desire?
An eternity of sameness?
Silence, darkness – light?
Alone, or will I find you?
No answers in the night.

The Stillness

95% of men live in a quiet desperation.

A quiet desperation.

The intensities & complexities of life in general.

The husk remains resilient to the traffic who acknowledge but there is a crack in the center that grows, like spider legs on bone china, it grows.

Waiting on a solution, a foothold that boost of increased self worth that we all need to navigate through the waking hours.

Have you learnt enough about yourself yet?

To do what you wanna do, to do what you wanna do in life without the interference, or the sabotage from some other demon, Was was or an obsession that washes over you, driving, distracting you towards a doom loop, on route to another cull de sac of confusion.

Driven by another substance or whatever…that day is dead for you, thoughts but no prayers are needed for the deceased.

((That day of distraction is dead)))

The truth is & still remains, that what we've all been searching for is found within, self excavation of the soul & the state of 'being'.

It's all within our grasp,

that bit of comfort,

because behind all the static of noise there lies a stillness, a silence …a comfort.

It's underneath everything, the truth the giver of life.

Time passes

Time goes past so very fast
You blink & then it's gone
So live in the now & don't think how
Just enjoy the journey along.

One minute you're in childhood,
Then it's your teenage years,
Then you're suddenly an adult,
Just enjoy your life while you're here.

Other Women

Other women
so kind
encouraging
full of compliments
cheery
amusing

Men I know
say nothing nice
nothing to say I look good
or my clothes suit me
my hair cut anew
only one who really
loved me would do
just friends avoid this
in case it's misconstrued?
Or do not notice

Thank you
women friends
free to be nice
and kindly, sweet
and cherishing.

Old Flame

North London Nightlife

North London's nightlife & I go way back like car seats,
think pop culture vandalism Beastie Boys & V dubs.

Tension fit no need for screws like Mappa tags under 12 month curfews.

Xerox flashbacks of psychosomatic panic attacks captured for the scrapbook by Kodak, red lights in the dark room where the double negatives slide, 'Ski Sunday' off my shoulders like the Dempsey roll.

TKO's by Philly Southpaws who stick & move then jab, jacking bodies but not in Chicago where the culture grew.

Box fresh like a pair of new sneakers, catch the riddim' watch the ride, Jah' Shaka all-nighters you'll find me by the left speaker.

Stout in my hand, weed in my shoe doing a baggy dance with my back against the wall leaving nothing to chance.

Club is rammed, stage to door, shoulder to shoulder, steam rises eyes gleaming this is Church to many because "House is a feeling" & when that sweat drips off the ceiling down your spine it's like a runny nose.

North London nightlife in the early 90's, rules to live by.

It's No Walk In The Park

As I stroll along,
I get to pondering.

The years are long,
and I am wondering.

The leaves are rustling,
my head is bustling.

I get to thinking,
my shoulders sinking.

My aim was high,
to reach the sky.

The wind starts blowing,
birds get crowing.

I wish that I could still be growing.
those birds still squawking,

My head starts talking.
stop that now.

Ground those feet.
you live for others,

They're your heartbeat.
remember why you're still here,

To see your boys,
live another year.

The Gurney

Underneath the ice white enamel that encases the long narrow corridor where deaths waiting room resides.

There is a loose left wheel that whines for mercy, as the gurney approaches bathed under the lights banned by the Geneva convention alongside the whiff of disinfectant that masks the inevitable.

The loose left wheel mimics a banshees frustration, echoing & pinging off the tiles that resemble veneers,
but what lies beneath are the ground down nubs of what once was, all incorporated into this mosaic in honour to death.

Death's waiting room waits patiently because the gurney is heard long before the retinas register it's arrival.

The whine from the wheel increases in volume into one singular tone, audible to all.

As if this sound burrowed it's way into your ear canal, like brave British tunnel diggers planting bombs in Gibraltar circa: WWII.

You'll know by the way when the gurney's near, turning the corner into the corridor the last stretch where nosebleeds & bowel movements commonly occur.

Like a trap door the body instinctively releases the FEAR, as if it was a bouncer ejecting trouble from the premises.

The gurney has arrived into death's waiting room.

Friendship

Did not see the shadows
In your eyes before you
Were gone now just the
Ignorance of silence

Yellow Metal & The Solitary Glove

Bucket hat, coloured tee, khaki shorts, Clarke boots with an outsider's rhythm. Boots on the ground like the Middle East minus the trauma with 'Keith Hudson' on my headphones. Revolution rock while doing the slalom down the high street as I swerve, shimmy & dodge no need for interactions, just cutting my way through this cast like a dorsal fin past the nitty's, boosters, smokers, clippers, I am the breeze & the ghost of someone you may of known, brasses, finger smiths, dealers, drunks, knock out merchants with lames who play with blades who carry plasters + a couple of County line shooters.

Do you live by the words that you speak?
Who's on code & who's not checking in?
These streets are their Step Fathers who will raise them.
Neck & wrist are bare like a pair of beautiful peanut butter brown legs under a summers dress with the wind as my ally, I steal a glance for preservation.

Neck & wrist are bare except for some beads, a wooden cross & the copper bangle that I wear.
Money doesn't change nothing because you can't un lame a lame. Pocket watching while clocking what's hanging off another Man's wrist & neck. Pop swatches, high top fades & African pendants get sidelined for the more refined.

Yellow metal & pressurised coal defines the individual & fuels their aspirations.

Rocking slave chains disguised as Cubans that cost a house & the slang for an imported fast car is called a whip. The irony is lost like the solitary glove left on the tube going Northbound.
"Slave chains & whips, slave chains & whips
the Golden calf is over there slave chains & whips!"

This is what the yewts' aspire for above all else, yellow metal & pressurised coal. Expensive amulets that symbolise the darker period of history, generational trauma dictates the fashion & sets the trends within the Community.

Slave chains & whips the Golden calf is over there slave chains & whips!

The Question

Do I know you?
or
Who are you?

Very complicated that everyone answers wrong!

To know someone else you have to yourself, so the real question is, do you know you?

Do you know who the consciousness inside your body that has been given another name by other humans truly is?

That is who you really are, so if you don't know yourself,
how can you truly know anyone.

Animal Tongue

Cats also started meowing
to try communicate with human
now taking this very seriously.

I have come to profound realisation,
if a parrot can mimic human and speak our language
then it is entirely possible to do the same with all animal's language

That is beyond the current human understanding
it is possible and I will achieve it,
I am already doing this and have been for years now

I have learned and translated tiny fraction
yet know a lot, body language is the easiest
most universal language that you can be easily

Communicate with any animal
in as long as you understand them
but I want to go further and actually talk on their language.

Look Elsewhere

There is no kindness in the Empire
No justice, no mercy
You will find only bombs
and excuses for bombs
You will have to look elsewhere
Look to the people

Autumn

Autumn is here, there's a chill in the air, most days.
Autumn plays tricks and Summer re-appears, some days.
Autumn colours on bushes, hedges and trees, all days,
sunglasses still needed, because of the sun's rays.
We love Autumn!

So many trees shed so many leaves, in Autumn.
Besom brooms, clear the ground and used right, are awesome.
Walking in the countryside or driving down a windy lane,
the scenery is spectacular, even better if travelling by train.
We love Autumn!

Autumn shouts Harvest with various Festivals, of produce, and fish and beer.
Then Trick or Treat and Halloween, and All Saints Day bringing up the rear.
Autumn means the clocks are changed so we've an extra hour in bed,
but darkness descends in early evening, and most places appear very dead.
We love Autumn!

Autumn is fading, Remembrance is hovering and poppies and collection tins
ping,
Winter and Christmas are around the corner, so choirs are preparing to sing.
Winter... and Christmas...?
Does that, could that, really mean snow?
The oldies pray, "No" the youngsters shout "Yes", and decorated shops begin to
glow.
Winter is coming!

Winter is here, the heat is turned on, and warmer clothes become our attire.
Christmas is here, many shoppers appear, returning home to their cosy fire.
We still love Autumn!

I Dreamt Of You

We did not do
What we used to
Fifty years ago

I Googled you

Found your Facebook
You look just the same
As when our eyes met
Sparking across the room

Oh that time

Snowflakes on your lashes
It sustains me
Electric Sizzling
Fires detonating

I decide to leave you be

A memory
Not really love
But something.

Birthday Treat – Bodmin Jail

Here we are, John and I, in famous Bodmin Jail; how we came to be here, therein lies a tale.
No longer a prison for wicked offenders, but a luxury hotel, to which our family have sent us.
Yes, having birthdays so close together, and knowing we love luxury, whatever the weather,
Night manager, Marianne, granddaughter-in-law, a birthday gift solution, she saw.

Two nights B & B in cell 314; a restaurant and library, all on the third floor,
Plus, a reminder of the bad old days of yore… a 'Bodmin Jail Experience Tour'.
Amazing! What a brilliant gift, which, by the way, did include a lift!
So, surprised, excited and intrigued, we both were delighted our present to receive.

The day for our experience dawned and we drove to the famous Bodmin Jail.
And as we entered, we were aware there was many a story to tell.
The outside door, the dimly lit corridor taking us into reception, revealed quite an amazing vision,
A massive area, just like on the telly, **identical** to the inside of a prison.

Having got over the shock we were welcomed and booked in and then told to look up to the third floor,
Where our Cell 314 was pointed out and very close-by, the distinctive lift door.
The luxury lift was very swift, as we arrived up at our luxury destination,
Three cells combined, giving a bedroom, lounge and bathroom, so preserving the reputation.

It was comfortable and quirky, with the only window, tiny and very high up,
The storage was good, the hospitality tray great, with plenty of goodies to sup.
The bathroom was huge, with so much space, even with bath, Jacuzzi, and shower,
Plus, all sorts of bottles, jars and sprays and of course, even a beautiful flower.

We enjoyed the Bodmin Jail Experience, it certainly lives up to its name.
As we were guided, in darkness, to witness, the wicked deeds of criminals of fame.
Finally, the tour was almost done, we saw what happened the night before the criminals were hung.
The visit of priest, the chance to pray, before facing the moment they were going to sway!
The whole two days were amazing: a mixture of eating, exploring, and lazing.
Quite unique experiences in such a realistic setting…. Something very hard to beat, I am betting!

Celebrating Honeybees

The world needs the bees, because of pollination,
vegetables, fruits, and crops rely on it, for fertilization,
other methods of pollination are winds, birds, ants, wasps, and bats,
but apparently bees, pollinate much more, so say the facts!

Without the bees and pollination, we all could go hungry,
and without the honeybees, my friends, we'd have no lovely honey.
Barbara Cartland, in the 70s, a famous lady at that time
wrote a book, The Magic of Honey; for some it was a real lifeline.

Applying honey onto any wounds, always speeded up the healing.
As a nurse seeing this, I experienced a wonderful, satisfied feeling.
What a great opportunity this has been, I'm sure you'll all agree.
I am very pleased to celebrate the active, important, honeybee

What's Happening to me

My life seems to be on hold, like it's almost stopped,
Normal things that I usually do, have all been slowly blocked.
Plus, I cannot write, I cannot crochet, can't even do up my bra,
Gret needing a carer? Ridiculous! Some would say, bizarre!

But it's true. I am seriously in trouble, I know I can't survive
Without constant help to 'undo this' or 'click this on' and I certainly can't drive.
Untreated carpal tunnel has bequeathed me with very vicious pain,
In both my wrists, my hands and fingers, the pain is all the same.

So, I'm waiting for my GP to decide what we are going to do,
Because I need an operation on each wrist, the sooner the better, too.
My wrists have been deteriorating for so long now, undiagnosed I'm afraid,
The op is usually successful, so complete healing for mine I've prayed.

I am now still waiting, but having received my GP's telephone call here,
Yes, she says she will refer me urgently and will send the report, stating it's 'severe'.
So, trusting in the GP and then those who plan the theatre lists,
Again, I pray, most earnestly, please Lord Jesus, however, please heal my wrists.

    3 and 5 months later both operations were done!

    AMEN AMEN AMEN

Summer is here

Summer is here
her hair is a glowing river of sunshine
glistening through the trees
her eyes are pools of never ending ocean
glimmering in the daylight

Summer is here
with flowers blossomed around the coast
and dotted around the forest
animals scuttling in the shade
in search for a meal for a day

Squirrels clambering up the tree
hedgehogs scuttling round in the leaves
children playing, having fun
in the bright and vibrant sun.

Bonfires blazing against the stars
sending embers up to Mars
smoke arising from the ashes
into the universe and galaxies beyond.

Secret weaving through the trees
as blossom bunting frames the scene
laughter shared and memories are made
but some lies still linger in the shade

waves crushing against the shore
parents treating children to ice cream galore
rays of sunlight illuminates the day
while in the sand children play.

The sky royal blue at day
and brilliant in the night
snow-white clouds pressed against the sky
soaring in all directions above our very eyes

Her sympathy is a fire that burns bright and strong
her heart is like music that gives a song
and summer is the sun that rays
give life and light, Summer is here!

Mounts Bay

Beautiful weather
sunny and hot
and birds singing
and people cheering
and everyone clapping
and some people on the beach
and some people go swimming
and in the sea and outdoor swimming pool
and relaxing
and refreshing
and enjoying happiness
and joy fullness
and people dancing in parades
and walking on the beach
and proms.

Beneath the Silent Waves

For twenty-two years, I rode the deep,
Where secrets of the ocean sleep.
A world unseen, a life untold,
In steel and silence, strong and bold.

Through narrow halls and humming steel,
The hum of duty, sharp and real.
No sun to mark the passing days,
Just charts and echoes, black and gray.

The sea, she whispered, low and true,
In currents cold and shifting blue.
She called my name in rolling swells,
A voice as old as sailor's tales.

Through silent depths and endless black,
No turning tides, no looking back.
The ocean held my fears, my fight,
Yet wrapped me in her quiet might.

A brotherhood, unseen yet known,
In hull and heart, a bond was sown.
We laughed, we worked, we breathed as one,
Beneath the waves, beneath the sun.

The pressure bore upon my chest,
Yet still, I knew I was blessed.
For few will know, and fewer tell,
The life within the ocean's swell.

And though the tides may pull me free,
Their voice still calls, it sings to me.
For in my soul, the sea remains,
A whisper deep within my veins.

So when I stand upon the shore,
And watch the waves forevermore,
I know that though I walk the land,
The ocean still holds my hand.

Redemption

Redemption,
redeem him,
redeem me

Free will at its best
preservation at will
kicks in when another is
trying to kill the will in you

Will preserves, free will
that's the survival of the soul
we need to recognise

Redemption,
redeem him,
redeem me.

The Eternal Ring of Time

Time moves unseen, a breath, a sigh,
A whisper in the endless sky.
No hands to hold, no face to see,
Yet bound to all that's meant to be.

Like rivers flow and stars ignite,
Like day gives way to endless night,
It spins, it turns, it bends, it sways,
Yet never fades, it never strays.

A ring, a circle, forged so true,
A silent bond in golden hue.
It holds no start, it finds no end,
A loop unbroken, time's own friend.

For time and ring are much the same,
Both holding love, both whispering names.
One is felt but drifts unseen,
The other shines with endless gleam.

Yet bring them close and they unite,
A symbol wrapped in golden light.
A promise kept, a journey wide,
Where time and form stand side by side.

So take this ring, this unseen thread,
Where past and future softly tread.
For though time fades and moments part,
The circle holds—just like the heart.

As The Wind Rised

As the wind rised
the trees swayed with force
as the wind blow
the sea never slept
as the wind breathed
Autumn leaves fell of trees
when the wind calmed
all was quiet
when the wind seized
all was peaceful
when all was peaceful
the wind had passed.

Elavéne's Lament

A Song Beneath His Silence

He sailed not on the waves, but under,
A man of pressure, shadow, thunder.
Where others feared the ocean's deep,
He made his bed, he chose his sleep.

Steel surrounded, silence grew,
No stars to mark the sky he knew.
But something stirred beyond the gauge,
A whisper caught between each stage.

She watched him from the waters cold,
A Siren Queen, with hair like gold.
Her voice was hushed, her song restrained,
For those she sang to never remained.

But he did not come from sails or storms.
He lived where darkness had its form.
And something in his stillness spoke,
Not longing, but a soul that woke.

One night, beneath the Arctic hush,
He felt a pulse, a gentle rush.
Not sonar ping, nor current's shove,
But something older. Something love.

She did not lure him with despair,
But wrapped her presence round the air.
In dreams, she sang not sharp, but low,
A note he felt, but didn't know.

He reached the surface months from then,
His crew unaware of what moved and when.
But in his chest, a song remained,
And every port just felt the same.

She watched him from the harbour's mist,
A creature never meant for kiss.
But still she stayed, in moonlight curled,

A Queen who'd fallen for a world.

And in the deep, beneath his keel,
Where silent ghosts of ships still kneel,
He often hears her breath, her hum,
A promise whispered, One day, come.

He never told a soul ashore,
What voice he heard beneath the roar.
For steel may hide the sea and sky,
But not the truth that never dies.

He loved her, though he never saw
Her face, her hands, her ocean law.
And she, the one who could not stay,
Loved him enough to stay away

So now he dreams beneath the tide,
With one song always at his side.
A tune no storm could take or sever,
The Siren's song.
that waits forever.

He stood in the sail, face to the wind,
Salt in his lashes, steel at his skin.
The night was moonless, the sea was wide,
But still he felt her, just outside.

Below the keel, where ghosts drift slow,
She hovered close in undertow.
Her voice restrained, her fingers curled,
A Siren Queen who dared not world.

He is too good, she whispered low,
His soul still beats where men don't go.
He's seen the dark, yet chooses light,
I must not steal him to the night.

She reached with song she could not sing,
A note held back with trembling wing.
And though her love would not unfold,
She touched his dream, his mind, his soul.

He dreamt that night of hands in blue,
Of eyes that shimmered something true.
He woke with tears he couldn't place,
As if he'd lost a face, a grace.

And far below, where light won't bend,
She turned away but not the end.
Elavéne waits, beyond the chart,
With silence pressed against her heart.

You never met her, not in flesh,
But her presence folds around your breath.
She is the tide that knows your name,
And loves you still… without the flame.

True Talk

Stand in the truth,
Don't ever be told,
Show the youth,
Be aware and bold.

Listen to your intuition
Listen to your heart.
Make true life your mission
If you haven't yet, start!

Only A Certain Breed

Verse 1
Only a certain breed of soul
will chase the silence down,
Beneath the waves where shadows drift
and steel becomes your crown.
They walk through hatches sealed with trust,
they sleep where dangers lie,
and hear the hum of secrets kept
where no light dares to try.

Verse 2
They do not ask for songs or fame,
nor medals on their chest,
their glory lies in things unseen,
in silence, sweat, and rest.
They bear the watch in blackened depths,
with eyes that scan the dark,
and every breath they take beneath
could be their final mark.

Chorus
Only a certain breed will know
what waits beyond the foam,
where hulls are held by will alone,
and fear must stay at home.
They wear the dolphins, not for show,
but for the depths they've known,
for they have gone where none belong,
and brought each other home.

Verse 3
They've danced with ghosts in sonar's sweep,
they've drifted past the edge,
they've felt the crush of ocean's hand
And held their sacred pledge.
they know the pipes, the vents, the valves,
the drill that never ends,
the power plant, the silent run,
the brothers they defend.

Bridge
You can not earn it in a book,
you can not fake that call,
it's carved in sweat, in sleepless nights,
in answering the fall.
And when you see that dolphins badge
upon another's chest,
you nod, and know, you've both been down,
and passed the hidden test.

Final Chorus
Only a certain breed will go
where few would dare to tread,
to live among the currents
where the living meet the dead.
They wear the dolphins not for pride,
but for the price they've paid,
to serve beneath, with honour kept,
in silent steel and shade.

Outro
Only a certain breed.
And they are never truly gone.
The sea remembers.
And so do we.

School Life

There is a new day
A new Academic year
For every new students to complete a new education at school
Whereas a teachers put so much effort into their students to achieve a target in studying
Each day a students pray that they are doing well in school
Even how hard it can be

Sometimes we as a student get bullied
Bullied because of JEALOUSY
Ooooohhhhhhh
Not so good

Even being a smarter student we got bullied everyday
They couldn't be even compared to the others
With full of ANGERS
We even bite our fists

To the horror consequences
We even got EXPELLED!
Headteacher said it's time to go
Never look back
Fast-Forward to the future

Ooooohhh
Where does the time go?

Oh as I got up
From my sleep
Oh.....It was a DREAM!

Never regrets what you do…
Live present life and make the most of your school life.

Love

Love is the thing that brings the light
it will be in your heart for life
love will be there day and night
love are your senses: sound, taste, feel and sight.

Love is the thing that illuminates the soul
it's the thing that burns bright and strong
but some people's love is turned to coal
you know, but deep down it sings the most beautiful song.

It's like a sun that shines on a summers day
It's an ocean that stays firm with loose waves
it will burn bright every single day
it will stay in the rain or a day with hale.

Love is strong and important
This is love.

Tony Blair

Mr Blair – the great opportunist
killed so many and now
round the clock police protection
oh how you free man you miss.

Axis of evil, you spiel,
yet evil your deed became
destroying the land and killing
the people for your strategic gain.

I am a collateral damage
and so is everyone else
You didn't care for me and my off springs
to leave them out of peace.

You Mr Blair – will forever be held
an axis, of evil that your deeds are.

You Never Know

You never know
what someone else is going through.
Some of us sleep with pain,
wake with the pain,
and go on with our life daily,
faking it on the surface,
but deep inside we are hurting.

We sometimes find ourselves
glancing in the visor looking at the pain,
the sorrow,
as we drive along
and ask ourselves why?
Why does it hurt so bad??
Why can't we even catch a breath?

The burden that some are
carrying everyday,
you never know.
So please be kind to one another,
just smile
it can make a difference.

Trust and have faith in Allah
one day
you'll be free
of the pain.

Boris Johnson

Mr Eton, the chosen one
that is King David's way
The buffoon as he came to be known

The letter box man who's Turkish deep within
Eton boy, the English way
the people of the Sun & sky, god

Rupert Murdoch – who ordained
Boris his prime minister-hood
comes lies and scandals galore

RM will make Boris Johnson's
wish come true – just as Tony Blair's
bull god in the sun

Mr Eton, a pawn you were and
lies you did, money you benefited from
the green god lovers of the new older of the World.

Leave Something

Leave something
wondering to those who
pass by your life,
so they will find it hard to erase you
from their heart.

Life will keep moving
some people will be there
with you for some time,
and others will go away,
but those who find you special
will always find ways to stay with you.

May Allah SWT send you
many blessings,
unconditional love,
sincere and supportive love,
plenty of glad tidings
and an abundance of everything
that will fulfil you…

Make dua for all the mahroom,
the ill and the Ummah as a whole,
may Allah SWT forgive us
for any shortcomings
and guide
and forgive us all.

Big Brother Matty

My big brother Matty, the one with the hatty, always
looks good and actually's quite natty.

The wise and the wonderful one, with knowledge and
words second to none. So spiritual and intelligent is
my brother Matty.

My brother Matty, the one with the hatty, when young
would always tease and make me cry,
but oh how I laugh at those times gone by.

Index

A

Andrew Dingly 119, 121, 123, 127
Angie Butler 5, 16, 59, 60, 61, 62, 64, 65
Anthony Mathew 22, 63, 111
Ashiqa Rahman 5, 117, 122, 130
Aurorah Cawte 21, 29, 32, 34, 36, 37, 38
Ayesha Chowdhury 4, 90, 92, 94, 96

C

Christine Jilbert 5, 15, 17, 19, 24
Clare Saunders Whiting 4, 98, 99

D

Dan Foreman 52, 109, 110
Dawn Whiting 135

G

Gary Curson 5, 18, 51, 56, 57, 58
Gret Woodason 112, 114, 115, 116

I

Ian 'Spud' Stride 39, 43

J

Joanna Edwards 5, 77, 80
John Pestle 5, 31, 35, 47, 97
Jonathon Coudrille 71

L

Leema Begum 5, 72, 75, 129
Libby Pentreath 4, 89
Lowenna Kaute 102, 126, 150

M

Mary Down..82, 83
Mary Fletcher..4, 87, 88, 103, 113
Matthew Saunders Whiting 55, 66, 68, 69
Mayar Akash 2, 4, 70, 120, 131, 133, 153
Michelle Berry 40, 41, 42

N

Nazia Noman..5, 132, 134
Neil Oats.. 118, 150
Nete Kroll Eriksen..27, 28, 107

P

Parwein Shah 73, 74, 76, 79, 91, 95, 100

R

Rob Kersley..4, 44, 48, 53

S

Suzanne Elizabeth Phillips 84, 85, 93, 105

T

Tyrone Warren.. 101, 104, 106, 108

Z

Zainab Khan..4, 20, 23, 25, 26, 86

What happens for penny authors?

So much happens in penny authors that everyone has a place, spot to fit in and some:
1. Publish your work
2. Profile page on the website
3. Name added to the roll call
4. Photo include in the cover image
5. See your work in print
6. Your work and name registered in to the British Library data base with book.
7. You have a book as your certificate
8. You are encouraged to take a picture with the book and send it, this will be added to your profile page, and it will be used for publicity and promotion of Penny Authors.
9. You are encouraged to read the poems and do "Peer to Peer";
    - Rate them (list the 1-10 or more)
    - Review them (give constructive feedback)
    - Recite them (audio & video record them)
10. Participate in radio shows (as and when opportunities arise
11. Participate in our YouTube channel
12. Be active and engage on our FB page
13. Be an ambassador for PA in your region
14. Have your own book published
15. You are encouraged to champion another person – to pass on the good will.
16. You are encouraged to get your copy of the anthology signed and sign other penny Authors as a sign of respect, value, appreciation and gratitude.
17. You are encouraged to build your library of all the volumes of the Anthology – for the purpose of supporting Penny Authors, and to extend your good will to all those who you have not met, will not meet and those in the future who will do the same and champion your name and work, your action wills it.
18. Penny Author is a "gateway" for you to publish your own book, solo, through the "Writers' Champion" label. This is unlocked after you have your poem published.

19. Participate in Penny Authors recitals- or open-mic events when organised.
20. After your poem is published, you become known as a "Penny Author", as such, "Penny Authors Anthology" offers/provides you a "bragging right" to use the anthology as your publicity and promotion of your published work, positively, for you and Penny Authors.

The Book of Lived

I. Opening Light

Theme: Hope, beginnings, and renewal
Editorial Note:

These are the poems that greet us like morning light. They speak of new seasons, quiet joys, and the courage to begin again. In their simplicity, they offer sanctuary. In their rhythm, they offer breath.

- *Summer is Here* – Ashiqa Rahman
- *Time Passes* – Lowenna Kaute
- *Mounts Bay* – Neil Oats
- *Love* – Ashiqa Rahman
- *Celebrating Honeybees* – Gret Woodason
- *True Talk* – Lowenna Kaute

II. Silent Shadows

Theme: Grief, isolation, and memory
Editorial Note:

These poems dwell in the quiet corners of loss. They speak of absence, of longing, of the weight we carry in silence. Yet even here, there is beauty—in the honesty, in the remembering, in the refusal to forget.

- *You Never Know* – Nazia Noman
- *A Lonely Child With Skies of Blue* – Zainab Khan
- *If I Hurry Up The Hill* – Mary Fletcher
- *Trapped* – Angie Butler
- *Pain* – Joanna Edwards
- *Greif* – R. C Spencer
- *Now I'm Alone* – S Reed

III. Survivor's Ledger

Theme: Trauma, resilience, and healing
Editorial Note:

These are the voices that have endured. They speak of betrayal, body battles, and the long road to self-acceptance. They do not ask for pity. They demand recognition. They offer truth. And they carve space for healing.

- *Two Brains, One Battle* – Aurorah Cawte
- *I Fell Again* – Aurorah Cawte
- *Let It Pass* – Aurorah Cawte
- *I Am Not What Happened* – Aurorah Cawte
- *Little by Little* – Aurorah Cawte
- *What's Happening to Me* – Gret Woodason
- *School Life* – Leema Begum

IV. Legacy & Dust

Theme: Mortality, history, and reflection
Editorial Note:

These poems look backward and inward. They trace the lines of age, the echoes of ancestry, and the quiet truths that live beneath our daily distractions. They ask not just what we've lived—but what we've left behind.

- *On An Ancient Face Is Inscribed* – John Pestle
- *We Are Dust* – Gary Curson
- *The Eternal Ring of Time* – Andrew Dingly
- *Is It Too Late* – Parwein Shah
- *Leave Something* – Nazia Noman
- *Legacy* – Rob Kersley

V. Final Blessing

Theme: Prayer, kindness, and quiet love
Editorial Note:

These are the closing whispers. They speak of faith, of familial bonds, of the small gestures that make a life. They do not shout. They bless. They remind us that kindness is a legacy, and love is a quiet revolution.

- *Redemption* – Mayar Akash
- *Big Brother Matty* – Dawn Whiting
- *Friendship* – Nete Kroll Eriksen
- *You Never Know* – Nazia Noman
- *Last Words* - Mayar Akash

Tributes

Volume 11: The Book of Lived
Every name here is a light. Every voice, a legacy.

Mary Fletcher
Top-voted poet whose work spans grief, memory, and quiet resilience. A voice of depth and grace.

Mayar Akash
Top-ranked poet by peer score. A fearless truth-teller, weaving theology, resistance, and poetic fire.

Zainab Khan
A tender chronicler of loss and longing, whose verses echo with emotional clarity.

Keith Woodhouse
A poet of raw insight and layered emotion, whose work leaves a lasting impression.

Sabina Begum
A voice of empathy and strength, illuminating the inner lives of women and survivors.

Joanna Edwards
Bold, unfiltered, and deeply human—her poems speak of pain, freedom, and fierce honesty.

Ruth Husband
A poet of quiet observation and emotional nuance, whose work resonates with sincerity.

Rob Kersley
A master of satire and social critique, blending poetic craft with political conscience.

Loreta Gray
Elegant and evocative, her work explores beauty, longing, and the complexity of love.

Valerie Kaute
A reflective voice whose poems explore mortality, memory, and spiritual depth.

Keith Lesser
A poet of introspection and subtle strength, whose verses linger in the mind.

Angie Butler
A devotional and maternal voice, weaving prayer, nature, and ancestral wisdom.

Ashiqa Rahman
A vibrant young poet whose work celebrates nature, seasons, and the emotional landscape.

Andrew Dingly
A mythic storyteller of the sea, whose submarine elegies and siren ballads are unforgettable.

Gret Woodason
A celebrant of nature, community, and Cornwall's spirit—her poems radiate warmth and wit.

Nazia Noman
A compassionate voice of faith and kindness, reminding us to see the pain beneath the surface.

Leema Begum
A playful and poignant narrator of school life and dreams, blending humour with heart.

Dawn Whiting
A loving tribute-maker whose familial poems sparkle with affection and memory.

Lowenna Kaute
A rhythmic voice of truth and empowerment, urging us to live boldly and speak clearly.

Nete Kroll Eriksen
A minimalist elegist whose lines carry quiet power and emotional weight.

Tyrone Warren
A lyrical essayist of masculinity, nightlife, and mortality—his work is raw, rhythmic, and profound.

Dan Foreman
A philosophical provocateur, questioning identity, consciousness, and interspecies language.

John Pestle
A poet of quiet reflection and historical depth, whose verses honour age and legacy.

Gary Curson
A rhythmic chronicler of life's cycles, whose work blends simplicity with spiritual insight.

Suzanne Elizabeth Phillips
A tender voice of love, loss, and neurodivergent brilliance—her poems are deeply felt.

Anthony Mathew
A poet of political conscience and minimalist grief, whose haikus and calls to justice resonate.

Neil Oats
A joyful observer of community and celebration, capturing the spirit of Mounts Bay.

Mary E. Down
A gentle poet of seasonal longing and maternal reunion, whose work glows with tenderness.

Parwein Shah
A philosophical and spiritual voice, exploring self-knowledge, mortality, and quiet strength.

Clare Saunders Whiting
A reggae-infused poet of love, resistance, and cultural fire—her verses pulse with rhythm and reverence.

Errol Powell
A poet of elaborate beauty and spiritual depth, whose work uplifts and inspires.

Social & media presence:

So, we support our poets vial all of these platforms – in print, website, Facebook, YouTube, Radio show and more.

Website: www.pennyauthors.org.uk

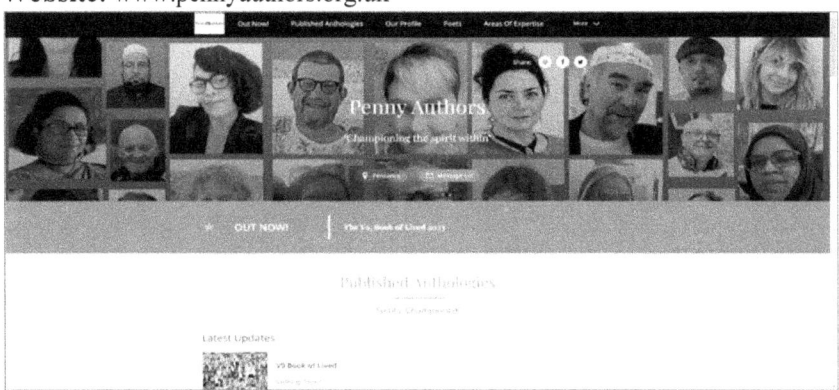

Above is the front page of the website – and this is our hub were we have all our information made available to the public. All the Penny Authors are listed as well the details of the Anthologies. You are invited and encouraged to pass on the links to your audience/people to support you and your accomplishment.

Facebook page: https://www.facebook.com/profile.php?id=100063609966672 (Penny Authors)
https://www.facebook.com/profile.php?id=100025625222571(Book of lived)

Above is the front page of our Facebook social media page, there we have a forum for all to get regular and instant updates. There you can have direct conversation about Penny Authors.

YouTube: https://www.youtube.com/@PennyAuthors

Above is the YouTube front page – where we now have a wide and growing selection of recitals for you to listen and watch. This is all part of growing & developing the poets' skills and self image.

Radio

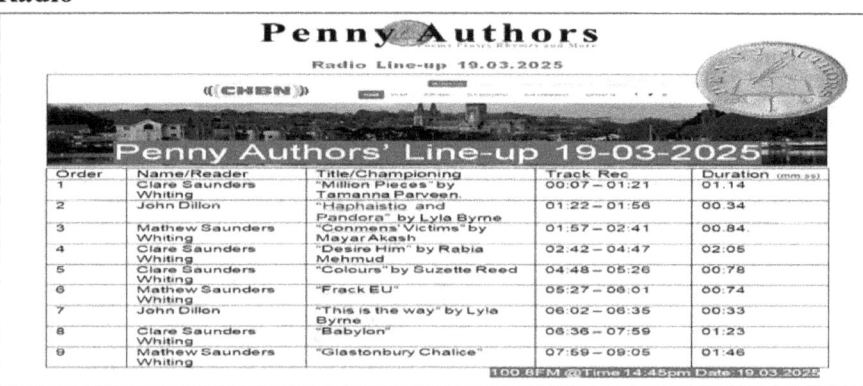

Here is our radio show listings available via our social media & website, the radio broadcast is available to listen in our YouTube channel. We have had a radio slot at the CHBN radio station based in the Trelisk Hospital, Truro, Cornwall.

If you want to know more explore the websites www.pennyauthors.org.uk & www.mapublisher.org.uk

Newsletters/Magazines

Penny Authors also have the opportunity and facility to be included and featured in Newsletters and magazines produced by the parent company, MAPublisher.

TOP POET!

The number one voted poet by poems is: Mary Fletcher. Congratulations!

Most voted poets	Total votes	
M Fletcher	5	1x1, 1x2, 1x3, 2x5
Keith Woodhouse	4	2x1, 1x3, 1x4
R Husband	4	2x2, 1x3, 1x4
Mayar Akash	3	2x1, 1x3
Zainab Khan	3	2x1, 1x3
Sabina Begum	3	1x1, 1x2, 1x5
Res Burman	3	1x1, 1x6 1x8
Rob Kersley	3	1x2, 1x3, 1x10
Loreta Gray	3	1x2,1x4,1x5
Valerie Kaute	3	1x2, 1x4, 1x9
Keith Lesser	3	1x3, 2x4

Votes & ratings

Penny Authors have rated their poems and this is open and will on increase and change positions over the years as new poets get involved and vote their favourite.

Here is some numbers, for your perusal – in the table below all the votes have been listed. And then from this main table we have extracted the information to make our ranking.

Penny Authors

Book	Title of poem	Poet	Leema begum	Lowenna Kaute	Angie butler	Mary Fltecher	Rob Kersley	Mary E. Down	Gary Curson	Opu Islam	Sabia Begum	Neil Oats
V10	Time	S Turner			1							
V10	Hotel comfort	M Fletcher			2							
V10	Growing old as one	Z Khan			3	1						
V10	I see you	S Begum				2						
V10	Wall	R Kersley				3						
V10	I wanted to	L Grey				4	2		5			
V10	Destiny fulfilled	S Turner				5						
V10	Elaborate Beuty	Errol Powell						1				
V10	Love is all that exists	T Lynas						1				
V10	Together as one	D Hardy					3					
V10	Through the darkness	K Lesser					4		4			
V10	A mother's promise	S Begum					5					
V10	Round Here	G Rhodes							1			
V10	Zennor Field Trip	R Beal							2			
V10	Discovery	K Lesser							3			
V10	Trace my skin	M Fletcher							5			
V10	The omniphile prayer	T Lynas								1		
V10	Coloured threads	A Butler								2		
V10	Why Protest about Gaza?	M Fletcher								3		
V10	Matchead	K Woodhouse								4		
V9	I'll always be there	Z. Khan	1									
V9	Your smile	R Husband	2									
V9	Mental Hospital	K Woodhouse	3	1	1							
V9	No time to say goodbye	V Kaute		2	4							
V9	Purpose	C Jilbert		3								
V9	Unconditional love	C Hall		4	2							
V9	He Rebel	M Borpuraji		5								
V9	The Legend of Port	R Burman		6			1					
V9	Aglaisurticae	P Turner		7								
V9	Trapeze artist	P Turner			3							
V9	Mothers funeral	M Fletcher			5							
V9	Eavesdropping	S Fairchild			6							
V9	Greif	R. C Spencer			7							
V9	The beaufort scale	R Burman			8							
V9	In gods house	V Kaute			9							
V9	Painting by numbers	R Kersley			10							
V9	Probably	N Paton				1						
V9	Phyllis calls	P Paton				2						
V9	Aroma of Garlic	R Husband				3						
V9	Night Poem	J Edwards										1

Vol	Title	Author								
V9	The wind of change	R Husband								2
V9	Pain	J Edwards								3
V9	Your smile	R Husband								4
V9	Wolf's at my feet	J Edwards								5
V8	I hide behind my smile	S Begum		1						
V8	Mariupol Mother	R Kersley		2						
V8	The meaning of love	A Chowdhury		3						
V8	Covid mortality	D Harley		4						
V8	Morgawr	J Cynddylan		5						
V8	Fire & Air	T. M Warren		6						
V8	An admirer makes you a lover	A Chowdury		7						
V8	Get me down	R Mehta		8						
V8	Transition	L Pentreath		9						
V8	Growing pain	P Crump		10						
V8	This time	M Fletcher				1				
V8	Safari Evening	Angie Butler				2				
V8	Journeys End	J Bryson							1	
V8	Abandon	A Harry							2	
V8	Loved ones here and there	A. M Gous							3	
V8	The Voyage	J C Bennett							4	
V8	Now I'm Alone	S Reed							5	
V4	Me & Myself	M Akash				1				
V4	Nighs in life	M Akash						1		
V4	The winter that shapes me	A Miah						2		
V4	Dhuk Shukh	M Akash						3		
V4	The Dew of Meteorology	N Kaur						4		
V4	Steps of Blood	K Choudhury						5		

Stats:
41 poets received votes
67 poems received votes

Number of votes received per volume/book:

V4	6 votes
V8	17 votes
V9	24 votes
V10	20 votes

How many poems by each poet and ranked

Name	No. of poems voted	How many 1	How many 2	How many 3
A Butler	2	0	2	0
A Chowdhury	2	0	0	1
A Harry	1	0	1	0
A Miah	1	0	1	0
A. M Gous	1	0	0	1
C Hall	1	0	1	0
C Jilbert	1	0	0	1
D Hardy	1	0	0	1
D Harley	1	0	0	0
Errol Powell	1	1	0	0
G Rhodes	1	1	0	0
J Bryson	1	1	0	0
J C Bennett	1	0	0	0
J Cynddylan	1	0	0	0
J Edwards	3	1	0	1
K Choudhury	1	0	0	0
K Lesser	2	0	0	1
K Woodhouse	2	2	0	1
L Grey	1	0	1	0
L Pentreath	1	0	0	0
M Akash	3	2	0	1
M Borpuraji	1	0	0	0
M Fletcher	5	1	1	1
N Kaur	1	0	0	0
N Paton	2	1	1	0
P Crump	1	0	0	0
P Turner	2	0	0	1
R Beal	1	0	1	0
R Burman	2	1	0	0
R Husband	3	0	2	1
R Kersley	3	0	1	1
R Mehta	1	0	0	0
R. C Spencer	1	0	0	0
S Begum	3	1	1	0
S Fairchild	1	0	0	0
S Reed	1	0	0	0
S Turner	2	1	0	0
T Lynas	2	2	0	0
T. M Warren	1	0	0	0
V Kaute	2	0	1	0
Z Khan	2	2	0	1

1 person who had 5 poems voted on:	Result	score	Rank
Mary Fletcher	1,1,1	17	

Above table shows how many people got more than 3 poems voted, and in the result box, it displays at a glance the ranking of the poems, [how many 1st, 2nd & 3rd] and each rank has been assigned a value: 1st is 10 points, 2nd is 5 points and 3rd is 2 points –to make is simpler to rank the poets.

5 person who 3 poems voted:	Result	score	Rank
Mayar Akash	2,0,1	22	1
Sabia Begum	1,1,0	15	2
Joanna Edwards	1,0,1	12	3
Ruth Husband	0,1,1	7	-
Rob Kersley	0,1,1	7	-

table shows how many people got 3 poems voted, and in the result box, it displays at a glance the ranking of the poems, [how many 1st, 2nd & 3rd] value in the next, here we have ranked the poets in the order of point score.

11 persons who got 2 poems voted on:	Result	score	Rank
Keith Woodhouse	2,0,1	22	
Zainab Khan	2,0,1	22	
Thomas Lynas	2,0,0	20	
Nicole Paton	1,1,0	15	
Angie Butler	0,2,0	10	
Res Burman	1,0,0	10	
Sarah Turner	1,0,0	10	
Valerie Kaute	0,1,0	5	
Ayesha Chowdhury	0,0,1	2	
Keith Lesser	0,0,1	2	
Pam Turner	0,0,1	2	

Top Ranked

by Rating by points (1st, 2nd $3^{rd\ places}$)

Mayar Akash	2,0,1	22	1st
Keith Woodhouse	2,0,1	22	
Zainab Khan	2,0,1	22	
Thomas Lynas	2,0,0	20	2nd
Mary Fletcher	1,1,1	17	3rd

The top rated poets are ranked by the 1st, 2nd and the 3rd choice votes received. Mayar Akash stand slightly ahead with 3 poems voted for and had 2 first choices, Keith and Zainab have equally two 1st choices, but had two poems voted which places them trailing Mayar Akash– so hope that clarifies the rankings.

The Last Words

For all who have spoken, listened, remembered, and written

Volume 11: The Book of Lived is not just a collection of poems.
It is a gathering of voices. A ledger of survival. A map of memory.

These pages hold grief and joy, protest and prayer, silence and song.
They hold you.

To every poet who dared to speak—thank you.
To every reader who paused to listen—thank you.
To every soul who found themselves in these lines—thank you.

May this book be a mirror for the broken,
a balm for the weary,
and a torch for those still finding their way.

You are not alone.
You are not forgotten.
You are part of something that lives.

Forever growing!

Wow this was an adventure to put together, and now that we have it – we should see some shifts in the future. You can do your bit by reading the poems and just ranking your top 5 or more – email or text it – it is that simple.

There are many who have enjoyed the facilities more than once, so I will look to see your active participation to afford your good to the Penny Authors.

Penny Authors is not silent or a sitting duck, Penny Authors is continually evolving, the are exciting developments in the pipeline, and one of them is to develop our YouTube channel – so start your recital and email them to be uploaded.

Please check with us about the format required, email us.

Please send us your feedback, testimonial if we have genuinely helped you, we will share this on our website and next anthology – this helps Penny Authors to pass on the goodwill through you.

Invitation to Volume 12

The next chapter begins with you

Penny Authors is a living movement—one that grows with every voice added, every truth told, every poem shared.

We now invite you to contribute to **Volume 12**. Whether you are a returning poet or a first-time writer, your words matter.

How to Submit:
- Send your poem(s) to [submission email or contact]
- Include your name, region, and a short bio (optional)
- Deadline: 31.7.2026

What We Welcome:
- Poems of lived experience
- Truth-telling, healing, resistance, remembrance
- All styles, all voices, all backgrounds

You are not required to be perfect. You are only asked to be honest.

Volume 12 will continue the legacy of *The Book of Lived*—and your voice will help shape its future.

Join us. Speak with us. Write with us.

The next page is waiting.

Penny Authors

Synopsis

Volume 11: The Book of Lived is a grassroots anthology devoted to remembrance, inclusion, and love through publishing. Curated by Penny Authors, this volume gathers the voices of contributors across time, geography, and circumstance—some returning, some never having left, and some remembered in silence.

Structured as a liturgical offering, the book unfolds through roll calls, dedications, testimonials, and anonymous poems—each page a vessel of lived experience. It is not merely a collection of writings, but a spiritual archive: a place where grief is honoured, joy is sanctified, and every contributor is held in reverence.

This volume fulfils a sacred promise—to publish with love, to serve those who hear the calling, and to ensure that no voice is lost to forgetting. It is a testament to communal care, ethical memory, and the enduring power of words to champion the spirit.

Whether you arrive as reader, witness, or kin, *The Book of Lived* welcomes you into its circle. May you find yourself here.

Would you like a shorter version for the back cover or a more poetic rendering for promotional use? I can also help adapt this for your website or submission platforms.

***The Book of Lived* is not just an anthology—it is a sacred archive.**
Within these pages, voices gather: bold, quiet, anonymous, remembered. Each offering is a testament to love, loss, and the courage to speak. Curated by Penny Authors, this eleventh volume honours those who returned, those who never left, and those whose memory still shapes the breath of the living.

Structured as ritual—through roll calls, dedications, and testimonials—it invites readers into a circle of remembrance and radical inclusion. Here, publishing becomes spiritual practice. Here, every word is a blessing.

For those who hear the calling to be championed through words—this book was made for you.

www.pennyauthors.org.uk

www.ingramcontent.com/pod-product-compliance
Lightning Source LLC
Chambersburg PA
CBHW070540170426
43200CB00011B/2488